The social history of Canada

MICHAEL BLISS, EDITOR

In times like these

NELLIE L. McCLUNG

WITH AN INTRODUCTION BY VERONICA STRONG-BOAG

UNIVERSITY OF TORONTO PRESS
Toronto and Buffalo

© University of Toronto Press 1972

Toronto and Buffalo

All rights reserved

Reprinted 1974, 1976, 1980

Printed in the United States of America

ISBN (casebound) 0-8020-1823-8

ISBN (paperback) 0-8020-6125-7

LC 70-163829

CN ISSN 0085-6207

Social History of Canada 5

The photograph of Nellie McClung on the cover is courtesy of
the Glenbow- Alberta Institute, Calgary, Alberta.

This book has been published with the assistance of a grant from
the Canada Council.

The original edition of this work was published in the United States
in 1915 by D. Appleton and Company and was distributed in Canada
by McLeod & Allen.

An introduction

BY VERONICA STRONG-BOAG

'WINDY NELLIE,' 'Calamity Nell,' 'Mrs Western Canada,' 'Our Nellie,' or, more simply, Nellie Letitia McClung personified Canadian feminism for the first quarter of the twentieth century. Her personality and career made her one of the most controversial of Canadians. As a campaigner whose slogan was 'Never retract, never explain, never apologize – get the thing done and let them howl,' she became the foremost practitioner of the politics of sexual confrontation.

Nellie McClung was an activist: a prominent campaigner in the successful drives for female suffrage in Manitoba and Alberta, a nationally known feminist and social reformer, the only woman at the Canadian War Conference of 1918, an MLA in Alberta, and the first woman to represent Canadian Methodism at a World Ecumenical Conference. In 1936 she became the first woman member of the Canadian Broadcasting Corporation's Board of Governors and in 1938 a Canadian delegate to the League of Nations. Sixteen books and numerous articles made her one of Canada's best-known authors. Working with press clubs and the Canadian Authors Association, she was a strong exponent of cultural nationalism. Today, her fourth book, *In Times like These,* survives as a classic formulation of the feminist position. As a Canadian, a feminist, and a reformer, McClung reveals much of the intellectual ferment of her time.

Nellie McClung was born Nellie Letitia Mooney in 1873 in Grey County, Ontario, and in 1880 with her family joined the great rush to Manitoba's wheatfields. During her lifetime Canada was undergoing major change: the nation was confused by suddenly overwhelming problems, both in burgeoning cities and in rural areas rushed uncertainly into the age of commercialized farming. The combination of large numbers of non-Anglo-Saxon immigrants and rural emigration, of industrial slums and rural hardship, of rising expectations and increasingly suspect business practices engendered explosive instability. Regional protest, particularly the west's resentment at eastern business domination, heightened the tension. Feminism grew in the midst of this social ferment, a vital part of Canadian society's attempt to deal with the newly posed social questions. The feminism of Nellie McClung and others must be understood as a special facet of nation-wide unrest.

The reform community was closely interrelated. The same individuals or their close associates promoted a great variety of change. Their crusades — temperance, urban renewal, social welfare, female suffrage — were undertaken while the Social Gospel of the Protestant churches was prompting the entire society to self-examination. Winnipeg was a centre of reform agitation. Nellie McClung worked with J. S. Woodsworth in that city's All Peoples' Mission. Her service with Methodism's welfare-conscious Epworth League further exemplified the commitment to positivism, efficiency, and morality which characterized so many of the Canadian progressives. If Canadian feminism's view of what women could do appeared over-optimistic, it was because of the suffragists' links with a semi-evangelical nation-wide crusade to purge Canadian society of its immoralities and make it a beacon to the rest of the world.

Little has been written about the female contribution to the Canadian progressive movement. Great numbers of women participated in every variety of reform activity. The Canadian community was almost unanimous in its attribution of a higher morality to its women folk. Believing this, women could quite legitimately claim a strong affinity for reform. McClung, like other Canadian women, viewed motherhood as a sacred trust: 'Women must be made to feel their responsibilities. All this protective love, this instinctive mother love, must be organized in some way, and made effective. There was enough of it in the world to do away with all the evils which war upon childhood, undernourishment, slum conditions, child labor, drunkenness. Women could abolish all these if they wanted to.'[1]

The mothering ideal was central to McClung's feminism. As traditionally as any of her opponents she regarded motherhood as the highest achievement of her sex. She believed that 'every normal woman desires children.' *In Times like These* contains no radical reinterpretation of the feminine personality. Instead, McClung's demand for women's rights is presented as a logical extension of traditional views of female moral superiority and maternal responsibility. Women must at last emerge from the home and use their special talents to serve and save the race. In emphasizing this particular characterization of women, McClung wrote within a familiar belief pattern, acceptable to both conservatives and liberals.

The suffragists rejected the Pauline doctrine of feminine inferiority. As women they made a long overdue claim on the liberal heritage of human perfectibility. Their campaign was justified at two philosophical levels. One was egalitarian, the demand for rights natural to all human beings. The other was essentially inegalitarian, based on presumptions of feminine superiority: only women had the spiritual and moral resources to reform society. This distinction was never fully clarified, and suffragist arguments fluctuated erratically between the two philosophical poles, the confusion hidden for the short term by the overriding goal of enfranchisement.

Dr Emily Howard Stowe founded the first Canadian women's suffrage organization, the Toronto Women's Literary Club, in 1876. Not until 1883 were its members confident enough to stand revealed as the Toronto Women's Suffrage Association. By organizing parades and study groups, by flooding the Ontario legislature with feminist petitions, this experiment established the pattern for other provincial campaigns. The formation of national organizations followed: the Dominion Women's Enfranchisement Association in 1889 (later the Canadian Suffrage Association), and the National Union of Woman Suffrage Societies of Canada in 1914. With encouragement from Ontario, campaigns were organized in the west beginning about 1912. By then suffragists had the powerful support of the major farm groups in Alberta, Saskatchewan, and Manitoba: prairie feminism developed in the most sympathetic of Canadian communities. The west coast crusade began in the 1880s and proceeded very slowly through a long series of petitions and marches. Reflecting the narrow regionalism of their community, British Columbia's feminists did little of the missionary work which characterized their Ontario counterparts. The Atlantic coast was still more conservative. Although the Woman's Christian Temperance Union (WCTU) of New Brunswick was very active in the suffrage cause, Maritimers were generally indifferent. Suffrage came slowly and with little publicity. In Quebec paternalism and traditionalism staged a last-ditch stand, preventing enfranchisement until 1940. Before the First World War Ottawa usually avoided the entire issue by pleading provincial jurisdiction. John A. Macdonald's abortive concessions in the 1884 franchise bill were repeated in other years, but it was not until the Wartime Elections Act of 1917 that there was sufficient support to pass even a limited national measure.

But much had been obtained earlier. Some women could vote in municipal and school-board elections. Many institutions of higher learning had been opened to women. Dr Emily Stowe's group supported the establishment of the Ontario Medical College for Women in 1883 and pressured the University of Toronto into admitting female students in 1886. Women typists, stenographers, and teachers were now taken for granted in the everyday work world. Middle-class women, newly freed from household serfdom in the pre-industrial, non-urban family, were particularly active in all these advances. The tremendous growth of the women's club movement before 1914 – mixing socializing and social service about equally – was the product of their first tentative explorations outside the home.

In the pioneering forays for equal rights the ebullient Mrs Wesley McClung proved herself well suited for confrontation politics. After she presented her reform credentials in the best-selling *Sowing Seeds in Danny,* it was almost inevitable that McClung should gravitate towards progressive circles when her husband, a pharmacist turned insurance agent, was transferred to Winnipeg in 1911. By this time British and American feminists were making frequent lecture tours across the continent, and the visit of Sylvia Pankhurst of the British Militant Suffragettes to Winnipeg in 1912 strengthened McClung's earlier sympathies.

In 1912 she joined in organizing the Winnipeg Political Equality League, an association which one knowledgeable commentator has called 'one of the most enterprising and successful suffrage organizations in the Dominion.'[2] Its creation was a direct response to the plight of women factory workers. To illustrate the urgent need for female factory inspectors, McClung had led Manitoba's Premier Rodmond Roblin through Winnipeg sweatshops. His procrastination hastened McClung's political involvement. Roblin's assertion that 'nice women' did not want the franchise brought a characteristic reply from the woman who would be the most energetic stump-speaker against him in the next election: 'By nice women ... you probably mean selfish women who have no more thought for the underprivileged, overworked women than a pussycat in a sunny window for the starving kitten in the street. Now in that sense I am not a nice woman for I do care.'[3]

Rodmond Roblin's blindness to feminine activism made enfranchisement essential. Unfortunately for him McClung had dimensions unforeseen by the government journal, the Winnipeg *Telegram,* when it characterized her as an annoying mosquito. Showing more foresight, the provincial Liberals endorsed woman's suffrage and thereby acquired for themselves an outstanding campaigner. McClung would later recall that the ensuing battle 'was a bonny fight – a knock-down and drag-out fight.'[4]

To publicize their case the Winnipeg suffragists held 'The Women's Parliament' in January 1914. This tactic, in which women replaced men as the legislators and men petitioned women for the vote, was an old feminist manoeuvre, previously employed by Dr Stowe in Toronto and the University Women's Club of Vancouver. The Manitoba feminists had been rebuffed in another suffrage petition just before they restaged this farce in Winnipeg; the premier had contended that female sensibilities would be outraged by the sordidness of politics. Like many anti-suffrage arguments this stance was, at best, paradoxical; for if women were inherently purer, as was implied, they might rather improve electoral conditions than be defiled by them. Nellie McClung had listened particularly intently to Premier Roblin. She mimicked and mocked his arguments for three packed performances of 'The Women's Parliament,' and the propaganda value was tremendous. One of her novels, *Purple Springs,* includes an only slightly fictionalized account of the incident.

During the following provincial election McClung addressed at least a hundred meetings for the Liberals. A contemporary judged that she 'unquestionably exerted a greater influence in the election of that year than any other person who took part in it.'[5] The Conservative party retained power with a reduced majority, but it had not seen the last of Mrs McClung: in the summer of 1915 she returned from her new home in Edmonton to help defeat Roblin's scandal-ridden Tories.

In Edmonton she joined forces with another prominent western feminist, Emily Murphy. Assisted by a Calgary MLA, Richard Bedford Bennett, Murphy had been instrumental in the passage of the province's Dower Act of 1911, assuring married women of legal inheritance rights. Alberta's suffrage campaign lacked the bitterness of that in Manitoba. As an ally of the United Farmers of Alberta, McClung's reception by the legislators was always cordial. While Premier Arthur Sifton was not enthusiastic, he had previously shown, in the case of prohibition, some willingness to endorse popular causes. The unimportance of traditional party affiliations in the province was emphasized by the vote on female suffrage in 1916: the single objection came from a French-Canadian member.

Like other feminists McClung favoured ending the party system. Long years of obstructionist opposition from governments of all colours had made her cynical about political parties and their principles. Her antagonism was also typical of the prairie radical. She ran successfully as a provincial Liberal in 1921, but largely in gratitude for Liberal support during the suffrage campaign. Her Liberal friends must have found her an uncomfortable colleague. While in the Alberta legislature she admitted: 'I was not a good party woman ... I could not vote against some of the government measures [the United Farmers of Alberta formed the government in 1921] which seemed to me to be right and proper, and I tried to persuade my fellow members that this was the right course to pursue. I believed that we were the executive of the people and should bring our best judgement to bear on every question, irrespective of party ties.'[6]

Unlike some suffragists McClung also opposed the creation of a purely 'Woman's Party.' Instead she envisioned a great body of independent, intelligent women who would judge political issues solely on the basis of the public interest. Standing virtuously above the political wars, but holding the balance of political power, women would have the decisive voice in shaping the policies of every party. This independence would only be possible, of course, if women had the moral virtues McClung ascribed to them.

McClung's activities were not confined to the prairies. She was on call to feminist forces anywhere across the Dominion. If the movement had a national voice, it was Nellie McClung's. An observer wrote, 'No Canadian woman has spoken to both parts of the Dominion as she has spoken. Women from the motherland have come to Canada to advocate the cause of suffrage, but their words have not exactly fitted the case on this side of the water. The need was for the awakening of a consciousness of reform from within, and not so much for advice from without. Canada in this matter as in others was intended to work out her own destiny, and the need was for leadership. Western Canada has supplied a leader in Mrs. Nellie McClung.'[7]

McClung was also aware of the international character of the feminist movement. She frequently referred to feminists in the United States and Great Britain and herself visited these countries as a suffragist leader. Her views on the violence of foreign militants are difficult to ascertain. Her comic sense and acerbic wit provided her with more sophisticated methods of attack than most feminists of her day and ours. Confident of mass support in her own region, she was never tempted beyond the impulse to use her umbrella on the obdurate Roblin. A secure home life provided her with the necessary emotional resilience for her political encounters.

The First World War was important in broadening the bases of the movement that women like McClung had previously stimulated. Early manpower shortages meant increased female employment in hitherto unfeminine jobs. The image of the sheltered female became more obviously anachronistic. The Union government, indebted for the support of the female relatives of military personnel after the Wartime Elections Act of 1917, and anxious to increase its popularity, was vulnerable to feminine demands. At the same time women's patriotic work gave governments a ready justification for reversing their position.

Manitoba became the first full suffrage province in January 1916, closely followed by Alberta, Saskatchewan, and British Columbia in the same year. Ontario joined them in 1917 and by 1918 Nova Scotia and the Dominion government had espoused full franchise. New Brunswick's women had to wait until 1919, Prince Edward Island's until 1922, and Quebec's until 1940.

In the United States the suffrage movement advanced most quickly on the western frontier. Except in the special instance of Quebec, Canada's regions were not as distinctive in their timing. Western feminists certainly had more support than their eastern counterparts, but Canadians agreed remarkably simultaneously upon the extension of the franchise. Their change-of-heart appears to have paralleled worldwide liberalization on this issue. Somewhat different conditions prevailed from east to west in Canada and from country to country, but there was a good deal of interprovincial and international communication. The shared experience of the war had been essential in overcoming the last entrenched opposition.

While she campaigned for the franchise McClung also worked for the Red Cross and the Patriotic Fund. Her support of the war effort was recognized when Prime Minister Sir Robert Borden appointed her to the Canadian War Conference of 1918. Armistice and enfranchisement freed her for involvement in other activities. In 1921, the same year that she was appointed a Methodist delegate to the World Ecumenical Congress, she ran successfully for the Alberta legislature. She was not the Dominion's or even the province's first female legislator — two women had been victorious in Alberta's

1917 election. During McClung's five-year term she championed temperance, public health, mothers' allowances, rural improvement, and women's rights. She also favoured birth control and supported Alberta's act for the sterilization of the mentally unfit as a means of improving the nation's health.

In 1927 she joined a group of prominent feminists to petition Parliament for an interpretation of the clause in the British North America Act dealing with Senate appointments. The judgment would decide whether women were 'persons' within the context of the constitution. The Supreme Court of Canada decided that they were not in 1928, but its decision was reversed by the Privy Council in October 1929.

McClung's interest in the development of an indigenous Canadian culture and her internationalist sympathies were both rewarded in the 1930s when Mackenzie King appointed her to the CBC's Board of Governors and she became a Canadian representative to the League of Nations. Through these years she continued to publish widely, to work for improved prisons, and to promote female liberation through liberalized divorce legislation.

In Times like These is a wartime attack upon female parasitism (the result of 'fatty degeneration of the conscience') and what is now called male chauvinism – a phrase Nellie would have liked. Within the grand framework of her theory that the rise and fall of civilizations depends on the intellectual and spiritual achievements of women – the war being the crisis of masculine society – McClung covers a sweeping range of current issues. Her style is delightfully incisive and aphoristic, rising to comedy worthy of Leacock in such passages as her description of voting ('If you had never heard that you had done an unladylike thing you would not know it') or the parable of an insatiable Roblinesque ox named Mike. Although the book is basically a plea for women's rights – the best feminist writing Canada has yet produced – McClung's thought seldom strays from her broad social concerns. Her feminism, as always, reflects the evangelical social reformer's perception of a civilization in need of redemption. She is a feminist because she believes that only women can be the redeeming agents.

Although sympathy for the urban worker had led her into politics, McClung's pre-eminent concern was the rural woman and her family. She always viewed the city, as she does here, through the eyes of a rural spectator. Characters in her fiction were either broken or repulsed by the moral and physical degradation they saw in urban surroundings. Unlike reformers committed to urban renewal McClung usually considered the city beyond salvation.

Her agrarian bias made it difficult for McClung to appraise industrial problems realistically. In her novel, *Painted Fires,* Anna Milander is an unfortunate immigrant who embraces trade unionism through indolence rather than principle. Her socialism makes Anna a dangerous purveyor of social disturbance, for she has rejected that inter-class co-operation which social Christianity requires. Not even shared femininity could make the proletariat comprehensible to the middle-class McClung. When the Winnipeg General Strike forced the socially concerned finally to choose sides on the urban labour issue, McClung opted for her rural preferences. Her reliance on Christian stewardship as an all-encompassing solution to the hard issues of urban-industrial society exemplified that strain of Social Gospel thought which was turning radicals of her generation away from the churches.

In this ultimate conservatism, however, she was quite repre-sentative of the movement she led. The followers of middle-class suffragists may have included representatives of the industrial classes, but support came more often from the insecure but still respectable agrarian and 'petit bourgeois' elements of society. The female labourer was unlikely to have either the time or the inclination to co-operate with those who were so obviously her economic and social superiors. Nor was the franchise viewed with equal interest by those whose poverty demanded more concrete remedies.

While unsympathetic to industrial organization, McClung was not blind to economic deprivation. Another wartime book of essays, *The Next of Kin,* fiercely criticizes land speculation, curtailment of public works, and the soaring cost of living. The First World War also taught McClung the possibilities of government intervention in economic life. After 1918 she advocated its extension through old age pensions, mothers' allowances, public health nursing, and free medical and dental treatment in the schools. Her social thought was not sophisticated enough, however, to deal with postwar industrial problems, echoing Mackenzie King's *Industry and Humanity* in depending too much on the power of Christ-like co-operation. Other feminists, such as the city court judges of Edmonton and Vancouver, Emily Murphy and Helen Gregory MacGill, would be much more comprehensive in their approach to the urban crisis. McClung's response demonstrated the limitations of the social gospeler and the agrarian progressive.

Sweated labourers of the type Nellie showed Roblin in Winnipeg were often recent immigrants. At the turn of the century settlement houses like Toronto's Fred Victor Mission and Winnipeg's All Peoples' Mission were almost overwhelmed by aliens from southern and eastern Europe flooding into Canada. These unfortunate people became the subject of much progressive attention both in Canada and the United States. At the same time as Asiatics presented 'the yellow peril' in the far west, the European foreigner was credited with the potential of swamping Canadian Anglo-Saxondom with his poverty, his immorality, and his breeding capacity.

Although they are muted in this book, McClung was not immune to such fears. Like the majority of suffragists she was middle-class and Anglo-Saxon, by birth and training a product of Canada's 'respectable' community. Yet her confidence in cultural assimilation kept her from that paranoia which often characterized the nativist reaction to immigration.

She was optimistic about integrationist forces, particularly those of the purer countryside. Many of McClung's fictional immigrants adjust rapidly and successfully to Canadian life. Still, a certain ambivalence emergences in her treatment of these people. More than a concern for their unfortunate condition, her sympathy is also a product of the agrarian contrast they present to the degenerate, and sometimes Anglo-Saxon, figures of the city. Helmi Milander, the heroine of *Painted Fires,* displays essentially rural virtues. Her redemption is both from her alien character and from the depraved city. McClung treasured the innocence of these newcomers while she desired to eliminate their cultural particularities. Purged and safeguarded by agrarian values they would form the new nationality she envisaged; until then they required the paternalistic attention of native Canadians.

McClung's nationalism revolved around her belief that the west could serve as a model for a dynamic Canadian nation. The traditional non-partyism, ecumenical Christianity, and assimilating abilities of the prairies could produce a strongly homogeneous population. The west's rural character would safeguard the morals of the nation, creating a way of life that preserved essential human values. Nellie McClung wanted Canada to be known as 'the land of the Fair Deal, where every race, color and creed will be given exactly the same chance; where no person can "exert influence" to bring about his personal ends; where no man or woman's past can ever rise up to defeat them; where no crime goes unpunished; where every debt is paid; where no prejudice is allowed to masquerade as a reason; where honest toil will insure an honest living; where the man who works receives the reward of his labor' (p. 97).

And, she might have added, the land where no man takes a drink. The campaign for national prohibition, led by the WCTU (nicknamed 'Women Continually Torment Us'), was the strongest of the early twentieth-century movements to redeem Canadian society. When she joined the WCTU in 1897 McClung had with some justification considered it Canada's 'most progressive organization.'

As the treatment of prohibition in *In Times like These* suggests, temperance people were more than the cranks we now consider them. When alcohol was cheaper than milk, when existence was often extraordinarily brutal and 'civilized' diversions unattainable, drunkenness was common. Later societies, more sophisticated and fortunate in the variety of their escape mechanisms, cannot appreciate the destructive impact of almost total reliance on a single opiate. McClung's childhood memories of ugly community incidents involving liquor were not unusual. With little ready money and few opportunities to leave the home women were most often introduced to alcohol through the violence it induced in their menfolk. Personal experience of social breakdown drove men and women into the temperance organizations.

Along with private tragedy alcohol was thought to cause public corruption. It was generally believed that the liquor interests paid heavily into Liberal and Conservative coffers. As liquor firms were largely centred in Ontario and Quebec the western farmer could easily add the costs of overindulgence to the other forms of tribute he paid to the east. Prohibition was the simple remedy to a massive social problem offered by a generation that customarily thought in terms of moral absolutes and was ignorant of more subtle theories of social pathology.

In the United States the causes of woman's suffrage and prohibition were united by leaders like Frances Willard and Anna

Shaw. Nellie McClung worked for similar co-operation in Canada.
For her, prohibition was to be the major goal of the newly
enfranchised. The application of women's mothering instincts to the
wider society would inevitably mean the elimination of alcohol.

Often the intellectual centre of a small community, the WCTU
provided a forum for the discussion of social issues ranging far
beyond the drink question. While it perhaps promoted near-paranoid
beliefs in conspiratorial forces, it also supplied large numbers of
culturally deprived women with opportunities for mental stimula-
tion. This process of 'consciousness-raising' through temperance
work, however imbalanced, was in some ways particularly fortunate
for Canadian women. Unlike their counterparts in the United States
they had never shared an organizational experience or group activity
comparable to women's work in the Civil War. It had taken
American women out of the home, had driven them to the podium,
and generally broadened their perspective. In Canada the impact of
the Boer War, particularly through organizations like the Imperial
Order Daughters of the Empire, may have been qualitatively similar,
but it was much less extensive. The temperance movement provided
Canadian women with new opportunities for social and political
action. Nellie McClung was not unusual in having first discovered her
oratorical talents at a temperance convention.

Through her novels and essays McClung, like Ralph Connor,
became a major propagandist for the prohibition movement. She was
modest about literary efforts which were conceived as instruments
of moral reform. Her stories often depicted liquor's tragic corruption, and *In Times like These* drink was as much an enemy of
Canadian manhood as the Kaiser's legions. 'Oh no, there was nothing
fanciful about the evils of intemperance with its waste of money as
well as its moral hazards. It was ever before us. We believed we could
shape the world nearer to our heart's desire if we had a dry Canada
and that, we felt would come, if and when women were allowed to
vote. We did not believe that women would ever become drinkers.'[8]

Nellie McClung had a very explicit picture of a redeemed Canada.
It was missionary; it was rural; it was assimilative; and it was dry.

When changing social standards and increased feminine independence allowed women to drink publicly McClung was among many
to be disillusioned with this apparent fall from grace. Her reaction
was the inevitable product of her mistaken belief in feminine moral

superiority. Before the First World War the alliance between temperance and feminism was probably mutually helpful, particularly in the fundamentalist west. However, by 1926 her temperance sympathies had helped to prevent McClung's re-election to the Alberta legislature.

Disillusionment had been unexpected. At the turn of the century Canadian suffragists had set out to create a brave new world. All things seemed possible. 'We were young and vigorous and full of ambition. We would rewrite our history. We would copy no other country. We would be ourselves and proud of it. How we scorned the dull brown Primer from which we had learned Canadian history! Written as it was from the top down with no intimate glimpses of the people at all. British history was a fairy story in comparison.'[9]

When Nellie McClung died in Victoria in 1951 she had lost many of her old ideas about the special characteristics of the female sex. The cynicism had been of long development. In 1926, not yet discouraged, she wrote that women still had monumental difficulties to overcome in a world of employment which paid as much attention to appearance as to competence.[10] Two years later she was regretting that the standards the world set for women were so inflexible. Women needed a harmonious home life in order to take on outside activities, but children could be cared for quite adequately outside the home. The basic ambivalence of her thought was revealed, however, when in the same article she replied to the 'new woman' who questioned the traditional child-bearing role: 'Children are not a handicap to any woman. They open up a new world to their mothers, the rainbow-hued world of childhood, with its delightful confidences and the unforgettable times when, all the world shut out, mother and child wander together through the world of books.'[11]

McClung never really came to terms with women whose major function would not be motherhood, nor did her analysis of working women make much allowance for the disadvantaged who had little but exhaustion to offer their families. She failed, as did the majority of American feminists, to provide modern women with satisfactory identity models. Instead, in a newly secular world and an increasingly permissive society, she left women with a missionary role which emphasized the centrality of the maternal experience. McClung's rural sympathies made her analysis appear ever more irrelevant in an urban age.

There was another strain on the practicality of her position. Despite her close social and political relationships with a number of men, McClung's arguments often have anti-masculine overtones. Men were frequently portrayed as aggressive, selfish, and uncontrollable. Women were their victims. This myopia is often an unfortunate corollary to the claim of female moral superiority. It leads to a type of reverse sexual discrimination that is one of the most serious flaws in the feminist argument.

Like Canada itself Nellie McClung did not develop a radical ideology. A mind formed by a Victorian belief system and a Methodist social gospel both of which emphasized the special attributes of women was limited in its freedom to develop. Neither a middle-class rural upbringing nor a nationalist's supreme confidence in Canada's future was conducive to a radical reinterpretation of women and Canadian society. In the first quarter of the twentieth century it still seemed possible for traditional remedies to create the world which feminists desired. If McClung was naïve in her reactions to drink, the city, and industrialism, and in her expectations for Canada and its women, it was a naïveté born of the liberal's belief in human perfectibility and a social Christian's confidence in the force of good. In all these assumptions she was a creature of her time and place.

Nellie McClung had already come a long way in her appreciation of feminine equality. The failure of feminism was not in McClung's particular shortcomings, but in her successors' failure to re-appraise the situation and avoid the same pitfalls. McClung herself was ultimately reassured by an appreciation of the larger perspective in which all things must at last be viewed: 'In Canada we are developing a pattern of life and I know something about one block of that pattern. I know it for I helped to make it, and I can say that now without any pretense of modesty, or danger of arrogance, for I know we who make the patterns are not important, but the pattern is.'[12] Nellie McClung was in her own way a social historian.

NOTES

1 Nellie L. McClung, *The Stream Runs Fast* (Toronto, 1945),
   p. 27.
2 C. L. Cleverdon, *The Woman Suffrage Movement in Canada*
   (Toronto, 1950), p. 55.
3 *The Stream Runs Fast,* p. 109.
4 *Ibid.,* p. 64.
5 Norman Lambert, 'A Joan of the West,' *Canadian Magazine,* XLVI,
   Jan. 1916, p. 266.
6 *The Stream Runs Fast,* pp. 172-3.
7 Lambert, 'A Joan of the West,' p. 268.
8 *The Stream Runs Fast,* p. 180.
9 *Ibid.,* p. 135.
10 McClung, 'I'll Never Tell My Age Again!' *Maclean's Magazine,*
   15 March 1926.
11 McClung, 'Can a Woman Raise a Family and Have a Career?' *ibid.,*
   15 Feb. 1928.
12 *The Stream Runs Fast,* p. x.

SELECTED BIBLIOGRAPHY

Nellie McClung's writings are numerous, including articles in such
major Canadian and American periodicals as *Maclean's* and *Collier's.*
Her two-volume autobiography, *Clearing in the West* and *The Stream
Runs Fast,* serves as a revealing social history of her period and a
fascinating portrayal of an outstanding personality. Her other books
include:

Sowing Seeds in Danny, 1908
The Second Chance, 1910
The Black Creek Stopping-house and Other Stories, 1912
In Times like These, 1915
The Next of Kin, 1917
Three Times and Out, 1918
Purple Springs, 1921
The Beauty of Martha, 1923

When Christmas Crossed 'The Peace', 1923
Painted Fires, 1925
All We like Sheep and Other Stories, 1926
Be Good to Yourself, 1931
Flowers for the Living, 1931
Clearing in the West, 1935
Leaves from Lantern Lane, 1936
More Leaves from Lantern Lane, 1937
The Stream Runs Fast, 1945

In Times like These was originally published by D. Appleton and
Company in the United States and was distributed in Canada by
McLeod & Allen.

OTHER SOURCES

Catherine Lyle Cleverdon's *The Woman Suffrage Movement in
Canada* (Toronto, 1950) remains the only comprehensive treatment
of the female enfranchisement movement in Canada. The biographi-
cal sketches of Canadian women included in *The Clear Spirit*
(Toronto, 1966), edited by Mary Quayle Innis, vary greatly in
quality, but for many individuals are a unique source. Using the same
technique but less useful are Byrne Hope Sanders' *Canadian Portraits*
(Toronto, 1958) and Jean Bannerman's *Leading Ladies* (Galt, 1967).
Two of McClung's suffragist contemporaries are well presented in
My Mother the Judge: A Biography of Judge Helen Gregory MacGill
(Toronto, 1955), by Elsie MacGill, and in *Emily Murphy, Crusader*
(Toronto, 1945), by B. H. Sanders. The founder of the Canadian
woman suffrage movement is briefly described in Joanne E.
Thompson's 'The Influence of Dr. Emily Howard Stowe on the
Woman Suffrage Movement in Canada,' *Ontario History*, LIV, no 4,
Dec. 1962. Other materials more specifically on Nellie McClung
and not included in the footnotes are: Una MacLean, 'The Famous
Five,' *Alberta Historical Review*, X, no 2, Spring 1962, and Margaret
K. Zieman, 'Nellie Was a Lady Terror,' *Maclean's*, LXVI, no 10,
1 Oct. 1953.

In times like these

NELLIE L. McCLUNG

Dedication I

Dedication II

Believing that the woman's claim to a common humanity is not an unreasonable one, and that the successful issue of such claim rests primarily upon the sense of fair play which people have or have not according to how they were born, and

Believing that the man or woman born with a sense of fair play, no matter how obscured it has become by training, prejudice, or unhappy experience, will ultimately see the light and do the square thing and —

Believing that the man or woman who has not been so endowed by nature, no matter what advantages of education or association, will always suffer from the affliction known as mental strabismus, over which no feeble human ward has any power, and which can only be cast out by the transforming power of God's grace.

Therefore to men and women everywhere who love a fair deal, and are willing to give it to everyone, even women, this book is respectfully dedicated by the author.

NELLIE L. McCLUNG

Contents

Chapter 1

The war that never ends

If, at last the sword is sheathed,
   And men, exhausted, call it peace,
Old Nature wears no olive wreath,
   The weapons change — war does not cease.

The little struggling blades of grass
   That lift their heads and will not die,
The vines that climb where sunbeams pass,
   And fight their way toward the sky!

And every soul that God has made,
   Who from despair their lives defend
And struggling upward through the shade,
   Break every bond that will not bend,
These are the soldiers, unafraid
   In the great war that has no end.

WE WILL begin peaceably by contemplating the world of nature, trees and plants and flowers, common green things against which there is no law — for surely there is no corruption in carrots, no tricks in turnips, no mixed motive in marigolds.

To look abroad upon a peaceful field drowsing in the sunshine, lazily touched by a wandering breeze, no one would suspect that any struggle was going on in the tiny hearts of the flowers and grasses. The lilies of the field have long ago been said to toil not, neither spin, and the inference has been that they in common with all other flowers and plants lead a 'lady's life,' untroubled by any thought of ambition or activity. The whole world of nature seems to present a perfect picture of obedience and peaceful meditation.

But for all their quiet innocent ways, every plant has one ambition and will attain it by any means. Plants have one ambition, and therein they have the advantage of us, who sometimes have too many, and sometimes none at all! Their ambition is to grow — to spread — to travel — to get away from home. Home is their enemy, for if a plant falls at its mother's knee it is doomed to death, or a miserable stunted life.

Every seed has its own little plan of escape. Some of them are pitiful enough and stamped with failure, like the tiny screw of the Lucerne, which might be of some use if the seed were started on its flight from a considerable elevation, but as it is, it has hardly turned over before it hits the ground. But the next seed tries the same plan — always hoping for a happier result. With better success, the maple seed uses its little spreading wings to conquer space, and if the wind does its part the plan succeeds, and that the wind generally can be depended upon to blow is shown by the wide dissemination of maple trees.

More subtle still are the little tricks that seeds have of getting animals and people to give them a lift on their way. Many a bird has picked a bright red berry from a bush, with a feeling of gratitude, no doubt, that his temporal needs are thus graciously supplied. He swallows the sweet husk, and incidentally the seed, paying no attention to the latter, and flies on his way. The seed remains unchanged and undigested, and is thus carried far from home, and gets its chance. So, too, many seeds are provided with burrs and spikes, which stick in sheep's wool, dog's hair, or the clothing of people, and so travel abroad, to the far country — the land of growth, the land of promise.

There is something pathetically human in the struggle plants make to reach the light; tiny rootlets have been known to pierce rocks in their stern determination to reach the light that their soul craves. They refuse to be resigned to darkness and despair! Who has not marveled at the intelligence shown by the canary vine, the wild cucumber plant, or the morning glory, in the way their tendrils reach out and find the rusty nail or sliver on the fence – anything on which they can rise into the higher air; even as you and I reach out the trembling tendrils of our souls for something solid to rest upon?

There is no resignation in Nature, no quiet folding of the hands, no hypocritical saying, 'Thy will be done!' and giving in without a struggle. Countless millions of seeds and plants are doomed each year to death and failure, but all honor to them – they put up a fight to the very end! Resignation is a cheap and indolent human virtue, which has served as an excuse for much spiritual slothfulness. It is still highly revered and commended. It is so much easier sometimes to sit down and be resigned than to rise up and be indignant.

Years ago people broke every law of sanitation and when plagues came they were resigned and piously looked heavenward, and blamed God for the whole thing. 'Thy will be done,' they said, and now we know it was not God's will at all. It is never God's will that any should perish! People were resigned when they should have been cleaning up! 'Thy will be done!' should ever be the prayer of our hearts, but it does not let us out of any responsibility. It is not a weak acceptance of misfortune, or sickness, or injustice or wrong, for these things are not God's will.

'Thy will be done' is a call to fight – to fight for better conditions, for moral and physical health, for sweeter manners, cleaner laws, for a fair chance for everyone, even women!

The man or woman who tries to serve their generation need not cry out as did the hymn writer of the last century against the danger of being carried to the skies on flowery beds of ease, for we know that flowery beds of ease have never been a mode of locomotion to the skies. Flowery beds of ease lead in an entirely opposite direction, which has had the effect of discouraging celestial emigration, for humanity is very partial to the easy way of traveling. People like not only to travel the easy way, but to think along the beaten path, which is so safe and comfortable, where the thoughts have been worked over so often that the very words are ready made, and come easily. There is a good deal of the cat in the human family. We like comfort and ease – a warm cushion by a cosy fire, and then sweet sleep – and don't disturb me! Disturbers are never popular – nobody ever really loved an alarm clock in action – no matter how grateful they may have been afterwards for its kind services!

It was the people who did not like to be disturbed who crucified Christ – the worst fault they had to find with Him was that He annoyed them – He rebuked the carnal mind – He aroused the cat-spirit, and so they crucified Him – and went back to sleep. Even yet new ideas blow across some souls like a cold draught, and they naturally get up and shut the door! They have even been known to slam it!

The sin of the world has ever been indifference and slothfulness, more than real active wickedness. Life, the real abundant life of one who has a vision of what a human soul may aspire to be, becomes a great struggle against conditions. Life is warfare – not one set of human beings warring upon other human beings – that is murder, no matter by what euphonious name it may be called; but war waged against ignorance, selfishness, darkness, prejudice and cruelty, beginning always with the roots of evil which we find in our own hearts. What a glorious thing it would be if nations would organize and train for this warfare, whose end is life, and peace, and joy everlasting, as they now train and organize for the wholesale murder and burning and pillaging whose mark of victory is the blackened trail of smoking piles of ruins, dead and maimed human beings, interrupted trade and paralyzed industries!

Once a man paid for his passage across the ocean in one of the great Atlantic liners. He brought his provisions with him to save expenses, but as the days went on he grew tired of cheese, and his biscuits began to taste mousy, and the savory odors of the kitchen and dining-room were more than he could resist. There was only one day more, but he grew so ravenously hungry, he felt he must have one good meal, if it took his last cent. He made his way to the dining-room, and asked the man at the desk the price of a meal. In answer to his inquiry the man asked to see his ticket. 'It will not cost you anything,' he said. 'Your ticket includes meals.'

That's the way it is in life – we have been traveling below our privileges. There is enough for everyone, if we could get at it. There is food and raiment, a chance to live, and love and labor – for every-one; these things are included in our ticket, only some of us have not known it, and some others have reached out and taken more than their share, and try to excuse their 'hoggishness' by declaring that God did not intend all to travel on the same terms, but you and I know God better than that.

To bring this about — the even chance for everyone — is the plain and simple meaning of life. This is the War that never ends. It has been waged all down the centuries by brave men and women whose hearts God has touched. It is a quiet war with no blare of trumpets to keep the soldiers on the job, no flourish of flags or clinking of swords to stimulate flagging courage. It may not be as romantic a warfare, from the standpoint of our medieval ideas of romance, as the old way of sharpening up a battle axe, and spreading our enemy to the evening breeze, but the reward of victory is not seeing our brother man dead at our feet; but rather seeing him alive and well, working by our side.

To this end let us declare war on all meanness, snobbishness, petty or great jealousies, all forms of injustice, all forms of special privilege, all selfishness and all greed. Let us drop bombs on our prejudices! Let us send submarines to blow up all our poor little petty vanities, subterfuges and conceits, with which we have endeavored to veil the face of Truth. Let us make a frontal attack on ignorance, laziness, doubt, despondence, despair, and unbelief!

The banner over us is 'Love,' and our watchword 'A Fair Deal.'

Chapter 2

The war that ends in exhaustion sometimes mistaken for peace

When a skirl of pipes came down the street,
And the blare of bands, and the march of feet,
I could not keep from marching, too;
For the pipes cried 'Come!' and the bands said 'Do,'
And when I heard the pealing fife,
I cared no more for human life!

AWAY back in the cave-dwelling days, there was a simple and definite distribution of labor. Men fought and women worked. Men fought because they liked it; and women worked because it had to be done. Of course the fighting had to be done too, there was always a warring tribe out looking for trouble, while their women folk stayed at home and worked. They were never threatened with a long peace. Somebody was always willing to go 'It.' The young bloods could always be sure of good fighting somewhere, and no questions asked. The masculine attitude toward life was: 'I feel good today; I'll go out and kill something.' Tribes fought for their existence, and so the work of the warrior was held to be the most glorious of all; indeed, it was the only work that counted. The woman's part consisted of tilling the soil, gathering the food, tanning the skins and fashioning garments, brewing the herbs, raising the children, dressing the warrior's wounds, looking after the herds, and any other light and airy trifle which might come to her notice. But all this was in the background. Plain useful work has always been considered dull and drab.

Everything depended on the warrior. When 'the boys' came home there was much festivity, music, and feasting, and tales of the chase and fight. The women provided the feast and washed the dishes. The soldier has always been the hero of our civilization, and yet almost any man makes a good soldier. Nearly every man makes a good soldier, but not every man, or nearly every man makes a good citizen: the tests of war are not so searching as the tests of peace, but still the soldier is the hero.

Very early in the lives of our children we begin to inculcate the love of battle and sieges and invasions, for we put the miniature weapons of warfare into their little hands. We buy them boxes of tin soldiers at Christmas, and help them to build forts and blow them up. We have military training in our schools; and little fellows are taught to shoot at targets, seeing in each an imaginary foe, who must be destroyed because he is 'not on our side.' There is a song which runs like this:

> If a lad a maid would marry
> He must learn a gun to carry.

thereby putting love and love-making on a military basis — but it goes! Military music is in our ears, and even in our churches.

'Onward Christian soldiers, marching as to war' is a Sunday-school favorite. We pray to the God of Battles, never by any chance to the God of Workshops!

Once a year, of course, we hold a Peace Sunday and on that day we pray mightily that God will give us peace in our time and that war shall be no more, and the spear shall be beaten into the pruning hook. But the next day we show God that he need not take us too literally, for we go on with the military training, and the building of the battleships, and our orators say that in time of peace we must prepare for war.

War is the antithesis of all our teaching. It breaks all the commandments; it makes rich men poor, and strong men weak. It makes well men sick, and by it living men are changed to dead men. Why, then, does war continue? Why do men go so easily to war — for we may as well admit that they do go easily? There is one explanation. They like it!

When the first contingent of soldiers went to the war from Manitoba, there stood on the station platform a woman crying bitterly. (She was not the only one.) She had in her arms an infant, and three small children stood beside her wondering.

' 'E would go!' she sobbed in reply to the sympathy expressed by the people who stood near her. ' 'E loves a fight — 'e went through the South African War, and 'e's never been 'appy since — when 'e 'ears war is on he says I'll go — 'e loves it — 'e does!'

' 'E loves it!'

That explains many things.

'Father sent me out,' said a little Irish girl, 'to see if there's a fight going on any place, because if there is, please, father would like to be in it!' Unfortunately 'father's' predilection to fight is not wholly confined to the Irish!

But although men like to fight, war is not inevitable. War is not of God's making. War is a crime committed by men and, therefore, when enough people say it shall not be, it cannot be. This will not happen until women are allowed to say what they think of war. Up to the present time women have had nothing to say about war, except pay the price of war — this privilege has been theirs always.

History, romance, legend and tradition having been written by men, have shown the masculine aspect of war and have surrounded it with a false glory and have sought to throw the veil of glamour over its hideous face. Our histories have followed the wars. Invasions, conquests, battles, sieges make up the subject-matter of our histories.

Some glorious soul, looking out upon his neighbors, saw some country that he thought he could use and so he levied a heavy tax on the people, and with the money fitted out a splendid army. Men were called from their honest work to go out and fight other honest men who had never done them any harm; harvest fields were trampled by their horses' feet, villages burned, women and children fled in terror, and perished of starvation, streets ran blood and the Glorious Soul came home victorious with captives chained to his chariot wheel. When he drove through the streets of his own home town, all the people cheered, that is, all who had not been killed, of course.

What the people thought of all this, the historians do not say. The people were not asked or expected to think. Thinking was the most unpopular thing they could do. There were dark damp dungeons where hungry rats prowled ceaselessly; there were headsmen's axes and other things prepared for people who were disposed to think and specially designed to allay restlessness among the people.

The 'people' were dealt with in one short paragraph at the end of the chapter: 'The People were very poor' (you wouldn't think they would need to say that, and certainly there was no need to rub it in), and they 'ate black bread,' and they were 'very ignorant and superstitious.' Superstitious? Well, I should say they would be – small wonder if they did see black cats and have rabbits cross their paths, and hear death warnings, for there was always going to be a death in the family, and they were always about to lose money! The People were a great abstraction, infinite in number, inarticulate in suffering – the people who fought and paid for their own killing. The man who could get the people to do this on the largest scale was the greatest hero of all and the historian told us much about him, his dogs, his horses, the magnificence of his attire.

Some day, please God, there will be new histories written, and they will tell the story of the years from the standpoint of the people, and the hero will not be any red-handed assassin who goes through peaceful country places leaving behind him dead men looking sightlessly up to the sky. The hero will be the man or woman who knows and loves and serves. In the new histories we will be shown the tragedy, the heartbreaking tragedy of war, which like

some dreadful curse has followed the human family, beaten down
their plans, their hopes, wasted their savings, destroyed their homes,
and in every way turned back the clock of progress.

We have all wondered what would happen if the people some day
decided that they would no longer be the tools of the man higher
up, what would happen if the men who make the quarrel had to
fight it out. How glorious it would have been if this war could have
been settled by somebody taking the Kaiser out behind the barn!
There would seem to be some show of justice in a hand-to-hand
encounter, where the best man wins, but modern warfare has not
even the faintest glimmering of fair play. The exploding shell blows
to pieces the strong, the brave, the daring, just as readily as it does
the cowardly, weak, or base.

War proves nothing. To kill a man does not prove that he was in
the wrong. Bloodletting cannot change men's spirits, neither can the
evil of men's thoughts be driven out by blows. If I go to my
neighbor's house, and break her furniture, and smash her pictures,
and bind her children captive, it does not prove that I am fitter to
live than she — yet according to the ethics of nations it does. I have
conquered her and she must pay me for my trouble; and her house
and all that is left in it belongs to my heirs and successors forever.
That is war!

War twists our whole moral fabric. The object of all our teaching
has been to inculcate respect for the individual, respect for human
life, honor and purity. War sweeps that all aside. The human
conscience in these long years of peace, and its resultant opportunities for education, has grown tender to the cry of agony — the pallid
face of a hungry child finds a quick response to its mute appeal; but
when we know that hundreds are rendered homeless every day, and
countless thousands are killed and wounded, men and boys mowed
down like a field of grain, and with as little compunction, we grow a
little bit numb to human misery. What does it matter if there is a
family north of the track living on soda biscuits and turnips? War
hardens us to human grief and misery.

War takes the fit and leaves the unfit. The epileptic, the
consumptive, the inebriate, are left behind. They are not good
enough to go out to fight. So they stay at home, and perpetuate the
race! Statistics prove that the war is costing fifty millions a day,
which is a prodigious sum, but we would be getting off easy if that

were all it costs. The bitterest cost of war is not paid by us at all. It
will be paid by the unborn generations, in a lowered vitality, the loss
of a strong fatherhood, which they have never known. Napoleon
lowered the stature of the French by two inches, it is said. That is
one way to set your mark on your generation.

But the greatest evil wrought by war is not the wanton
destruction of life and property, sinful though it is; it is not even the
lowered vitality of succeeding generations, though that is attended
by appalling injury to the moral nature – the real iniquity of war is
that it sets aside the arbitrament of right and justice, and looks to
brute force for its verdict!

In the first days of panic, pessimism broke out among us, and we
cried in our despair that our civilization had failed, that Christianity
had broken down, and that God had forgotten the world. It seemed
like it at first. But now a wiser and better vision has come to us, and
we know that Christianity has not failed, for it is not fair to impute
failure to something which has never been tried. Civilization has
failed. Art, music, and culture have failed, and we know now that
underneath the thin veneer of civilization, unregenerate man is still a
savage; and we see now, what some have never seen before, that
unless a civilization is built upon love, and mutual trust, it must
always end in disaster, such as this. Up to August fourth, we often
said that war was impossible between Christian nations. We still say
so, but we know more now than we did then. We know now that
there are no Christian nations.

Oh, yes. I know the story. It was a beautiful story and a beautiful
picture. The black prince of Abyssinia asked the young Queen of
England what was the secret of England's glory and she pointed to
the 'open Bible.'

The dear Queen of sainted memory was wrong. She judged her
nation by the standard of her own pure heart. England did not draw
her policy from the open Bible when in 1840 she forced the opium
traffic on the Chinese. England does not draw her policy from the
open Bible when she takes revenues from the liquor traffic, which
works such irreparable ruin to countless thousands of her people.
England does not draw her policy from the open Bible when she
denies her women the rights of citizens, when women are refused
degrees after passing examinations, when lower pay is given women
for the same work than if it were done by men. Would this be

tolerated if it were really so that we were a Christian nation? God abominates a false balance, and delights in a just weight.

No, the principles of Christ have not yet been applied to nations. We have only Christian people. You will see that in a second, if you look at the disparity that there is between our conceptions of individual duty and national duty. Take the case of the heathen — the people whom we in our large-handed, superior way call the heathen. Individually we believe it is our duty to send missionaries to them to convert them into Christians. Nationally we send armies upon them (if necessary) and convert them into customers! Individually we say: 'We will send you our religion.' Nationally: 'We will send you goods, and we'll make you take them — we need the money!' Think of the bitter irony of a boat leaving a Christian port loaded with missionaries upstairs and rum below, both bound for the same place and for the same people — both for the heathen 'with our comp'ts.'

Individually we know it is wrong to rob anyone. Yet the state robs freely, openly, and unashamed, by unjust taxation, by the legalized liquor traffic, by imposing unjust laws upon at least one half of the people. We wonder at the disparity between our individual ideals and the national ideal, but when you remember that the national ideals have been formed by one half of the world — and not the more spiritual half — it is not so surprising. Our national policy is the result of male statecraft.

There is a curative power in human life just as there is in nature. When the pot boils — it boils over. Evils cure themselves eventually. But it is a long hard way. Yet it is the way humanity has always had to learn. Christ realized that when he looked down at Jerusalem, and wept over it: 'O Jerusalem, Jerusalem, how often I would have gathered you, as a hen gathereth her chickens under her wings, but *you would not.*' That was the trouble then, and it has been the trouble ever since. Humanity has to travel a hard road to wisdom, and it has to travel it with bleeding feet.

But it is getting its lessons now — and paying double first-class rates for its tuition!

Chapter 3

What do women think of war? (not that it matters)

Bands in the street, and resounding cheers,
And honor to him whom the army led!
But his mother moans thro' her blinding tears —
'My boy is dead — is dead!'

'MADAM,' said Charles XI of Sweden to his wife when she appealed to him for mercy to some prisoner, 'I married you to give me children, not to give me advice.' That was said a long time ago, and the haughty old Emperor put it rather crudely, but he put it straight. This is still the attitude of the world towards women. That men are human beings, but women are women, with one reason for their existence, has long been the dictum of the world.

More recent philosophers have been more adroit – they have sought to soften the blow, and so they palaver the women by telling them what a tremendous power they are for good. They quote the men who have said: 'All that I am my mother made me.' They also quote that old iniquitous lie, about the hand that rocks the cradle ruling the world.

For a long time men have been able to hush women up by these means; and many women have gladly allowed themselves to be deceived. Sometimes when a little child goes driving with his father he is allowed to hold the ends of the reins, and encouraged to believe that he is driving, and it works quite well with a very small child. Women have been deceived in the same way into believing that they are the controlling factor in the world. Here and there, there have been doubters among women who have said: 'If it be true that the hand that rocks the cradle rules the world, how comes the liquor traffic and the white slave traffic to prevail among us unchecked? Do women wish for these things? Do the gentle mothers whose hands rule the world declare in favor of these things?' Every day the number of doubters has increased, and now women everywhere realize that a bad old lie has been put over on them for years. The hand that rocks the cradle does not rule the world. If it did, human life would be held dearer and the world would be a sweeter, cleaner, safer place than it is now!

Women are naturally the guardians of the race, and every normal woman desires children. Children are not a handicap in the race of life either, they are an inspiration. We hear too much about the burden of motherhood and too little of its benefits. The average child does well for his parents, and teaches them many things. Bless his little soft hands – he broadens our outlook, quickens our sympathies, and leads us, if we will but let him, into all truth. A child pays well for his board and keep.

Deeply rooted in every woman's heart is the love and care of children. A little girl's first toy is a doll, and so, too, her first great

sorrow is when her doll has its eyes poked out by her little brother.
Dolls have suffered many things at the hands of their maternal
uncles.

> There, little girl, don't cry,
> They have broken your doll, I know,

contains in it the universal note of woman's woe!

But just as the woman's greatest sorrow has come through her
children, so has her greatest development. Women learned to cook,
so that their children might be fed; they learned to sew that their
children might be clothed, and women are learning to think so that
their children may be guided.

Since the war broke out women have done a great deal of
knitting. Looking at this great army of women struggling with rib
and back seam, some have seen nothing in it but a 'fad' which has
supplanted for the time tatting and bridge. But it is more than that.
It is the desire to help, to care for, to minister; it is the same spirit
which inspires our nurses to go out and bind up the wounded and
care for the dying. The woman's outlook on life is to save, to care
for, to help. Men make wounds and women bind them up, and so
the women, with their hearts filled with love and sorrow, sit in their
quiet homes and knit.

> Comforter — they call it — yes —
> So it is for my distress,
> For it gives my restless hands
> Blessed work. God understands
> How we women yearn to be
> Doing something ceaselessly.

Women have not only been knitting — they have been thinking.
Among other things they have thought about the German women,
those faithful, patient, homeloving, obedient women, who never
interfere in public affairs, nor question man's ruling. The Kaiser says
women have only two concerns in life, cooking and children, and the
German women have accepted his dictum. They are good cooks and
faithful nurses to their children.

According to the theories of the world, the sons of such women
should be the gentlest men on earth. Their home has been so sacred,

and well-kept; their mother has been so gentle, patient and unworldly — she has never lowered the standard of her womanhood by asking to vote, or to mingle in the 'hurly burly' of politics. She has been humble, and loving, and always hoped for the best.

According to the theories of the world, the gentle sons of gentle mothers will respect and reverence all womankind everywhere. Yet, we know that in the invasion of Belgium, the German soldiers made a shield of Belgian women and children in front of their army; no child was too young, no woman too old, to escape their cruelty; no mother's prayers, no child's appeal could stay their fury! These chivalrous sons of gentle, loving mothers marched through the land of Belgium, their nearest neighbor, leaving behind them smoking trails of ruin, black as their own hard hearts!

What, then, is the matter with the theory? Nothing, except that there is nothing in it — it will not work. Women who set a low value on themselves make life hard for all women. The German woman's ways have been ways of pleasantness, but her paths have not been paths of peace; and now, women everywhere are thinking of her, rather bitterly. Her peaceful, humble, patient ways have suddenly ceased to appear virtuous in our eyes and we see now, it is not so much a woman's duty to bring children into the world, as to see what sort of a world she is bringing them into, and what their contribution will be to it. Bertha Krupp has made good guns and the German women have raised good soldiers — if guns and soldiers can be called 'good' — and between them they have manned the most terrible and destructive war machine that the world has ever known. We are not grateful to either of them.

The nimble fingers of the knitting women are transforming balls of wool into socks and comforters, but even a greater change is being wrought in their own hearts. Into their gentle souls have come bitter thoughts of rebellion. They realize now how little human life is valued, as opposed to the greed and ambition of nations. They think bitterly of Napoleon's utterance on the subject of women — that the greatest woman in the world is the one who brings into the world the greatest number of sons; they also remember that he said that a boy could stop a bullet as well as a man, and that God is on the side of the heaviest artillery. From these three statements they get the military idea of women, children, and God, and the heart of the knitting woman recoils in horror from the cold brutality of it all.

They realize now something of what is back of all the opposition to the woman's advancement into all lines of activity and a share in government.

Women are intended for two things, to bring children into the world and to make men comfortable, and then they must keep quiet and if their hearts break with grief, let them break quietly – that's all. No woman is so unpopular as the noisy woman who protests against these things.

The knitting women know now why the militant suffragettes broke windows and destroyed property, and went to jail for it joyously, and without a murmur – it was the protest of brave women against the world's estimate of woman's position. It was the world-old struggle for liberty. The knitting women remember now with shame and sorrow that they have said hard things about the suffragettes, and thought they were unwomanly and hysterical. Now they know that womanliness, and peaceful gentle ways, prayers, petitions and tears have long been tried but are found wanting; and now they know that these brave women in England, maligned, ridiculed, persecuted, as they were, have been fighting every woman's battle, fighting for the recognition of human life, and the mother's point of view. Many of the knitting women have seen a light shine around their pathway, as they have passed down the road from the heel to the toe, and they know now that the explanation cannot be accepted any longer that the English women are 'crazy.' That has been offered so often and been accepted.

Crazy! That's such an easy way to explain actions which we do not understand. Crazy! and it gives such a delightful thrill of sanity to the one who says it – such a pleasurable flash of superiority!

Oh, no, they have not been crazy, unless acts of heroism and suffering for the sake of others can be described as crazy! The knitting women wish now that there had been 'crazy' women in Germany to direct the thought of the nation to the brutality of the military system, to have aroused the women to struggle for a human civilization, instead of a masculine civilization such as they have now. They would have fared badly of course, even worse than the women in England, but they are faring badly now, and to what purpose? The women of Belgium have fared badly. After all, the greatest thing in life is not to live comfortably – it is to live honorably, and when that becomes impossible, to die honorably!

The woman who knits is thinking sadly of the glad days of peace, now unhappily gone by, when she was so sure it was her duty to bring children into the world. She thinks of the glad rapture with which she looked into the sweet face of her first-born twenty years ago — the brave lad who went with the first contingent, and is now at the front. She was so sure then that she had done a noble thing in giving this young life to the world. He was to have been a great doctor, a great healer, one who bound up wounds, and make weak men strong — and now — in the trenches, he stands, this lad of hers, with the weapons of death in his hands, with bitter hatred in his heart, not binding wounds, but making them, sending poor human beings out in the dark to meet their Maker, unprepared, surrounded by sights and sounds that must harden his heart or break it. Oh! her sunny-hearted lad! So full of love and tenderness and pity, so full of ambition and high resolves and noble impulses, he is dead — dead already — and in his place there stands 'private 355,' a man of hate, a man of blood! Many a time the knitting has to be laid aside, for the bitter tears blur the stitches.

The woman who knits thinks of all this and now she feels that she who brought this boy into the world, who is responsible for his existence, has some way been to blame. Is life really such a boon that any should crave it? Do we really confer a favor on the innocent little souls we bring into the world, or do we owe them an apology?

She thinks now of Abraham's sacrifice, when he was willing at God's command to offer his dearly beloved son on the altar; and now she knows it was not so hard for Abraham, for he knew it was God who asked it, and he had God's voice to guide him! Abraham was sure, but about this — who knows?

Then she thinks of the little one who dropped out of the race before it was well begun, and of the inexplicable smile of peace which lay on his small white face, that day, so many years ago now, when they laid him away with such sorrow, and such agony of loss. She understands now why the little one smiled, while all around him wept.

And she thinks enviously of her neighbor across the way, who had no son to give, the childless woman for whom in the old days she felt so sorry, but whom now she envies. She is the happiest woman of all — so thinks the knitting woman, as she sits alone in her quiet house; for thoughts can grow very bitter when the house is still and the boyish voice is heard no more shouting, 'Mother' in the hall.

There, little girl, don't cry!
They have broken your heart, I know.

Chapter 4

Should women think?

A woman, a spaniel, a walnut tree,
The more you beat 'em, the better they be.

From *Proverbs of All Nations*

A woman is not a person in matters of rights and privileges, but she is a person in matters of pains and penalties.

From the Common Law of England

No woman, idiot, lunatic, or criminal shall vote.

From the Election Act of the Dominion of Canada

MARY AND MARTHA were sisters, and one day they had a quarrel,
which goes to show that sisters in Bible times were much the same as
now. Mary and Martha had a different attitude toward life. Martha
was a housekeeper — she reveled in housecleaning — she had a
perfect mania for sweeping and dusting. Mary was a thinker. She
looked beyond the work, and saw something better and more
important, something more abiding and satisfying.

When Jesus came to their home to visit, Mary sat at his feet and
listened. She fed her soul, and in her sheer joy she forgot that there
were dirty dishes in all the world; she forgot that ever people grew
hungry, or floors became dusty; she forgot everything only the joy
of his presence. Martha never forgot. All days were alike to Martha,
only of course Monday was washday. The visit of the Master to
Martha meant another place at the table, and another plate to be
washed. Truly feminine was Martha, much commended in certain
circles today. She looked well to the needs of her family, physical
needs, that is, for she recognized no other. Martha not only liked to
work herself, but she liked to see other people work; so when Mary
went and sat at the Master's feet, while the dishes were yet
unwashed, Martha complained about it.

'Lord, make Mary come and help me!' she said. The story says
Martha was wearied with much serving. Martha had cooked and
served an elaborate meal, and elaborate meals usually do make
people cross either before or after. Christ gently reproved her. 'Mary
hath chosen the better part.'

Just here let us say something in Mary's favor. Martha by her
protest against Mary's behavior on this particular occasion, ex-
onerates Mary from the general charge of laziness which is often
made against her. If Mary had been habitually lazy, Martha would
have long since ceased to expect any help from her, but it seems
pretty certain that Mary was generally on the job. Trivial little
incident, is it not? Strange that it should find a place in the sacred
record. But if Christ's mission on earth had any meaning at all, it was
to teach this very lesson that the things which are not seen are
greater than the things which are seen — that the spiritual is greater
than the temporal. The life is more than meat and the body is more
than raiment.

Martha has a long line of weary, backaching, footsore successors.
Indeed there is a strain of Martha in all of us; we worry more over a

stain in the carpet than a stain on the soul; we bestow more thought on the choice of hats than on the choice of friends; we tidy up bureau drawers, sometimes, when we should be tidying up the inner recesses of our mind and soul; we clean up the attic and burn up the rubbish which has accumulated there, every spring, whether it needs it or not. But when do we appoint a housecleaning day for the soul, when do we destroy all the worn-out prejudices and beliefs which belong to a day gone by?

Mary did take the better part, for she laid hold on the things which are spiritual. Mary had learned the great truth that it is not the house you live in or the food you eat, or the clothes you wear that make you rich, but it is the thoughts you think. Christ put it well when he said, 'Mary hath chosen the better part.' Life is a choice every day. Every day we choose between the best and the second best, if we are choosing wisely. It is not generally a choice between good and bad — that is too easy. The choice in life is more subtle than that, and not so easily decided. The good is the greatest rival of the best.

Sometimes we would like to take both the best and the second best, but that is not according to the rules of the game. You take your choice and leave the rest. Every gain in life means a corresponding loss; development in one part means a shrinkage in some other. Wild wheat is small and hard, quite capable of looking after itself, but its heads contain only a few small kernels. Cultivated wheat has lost its hardiness and its self-reliance, but its heads are filled with large kernels which feed the nation. There has been a great gain in usefulness, by cultivation, with a corresponding loss in hardiness. When riches are increased, so also are anxieties and cares. Life is full of compensation.

So we ask, in all seriousness, and in no spirit of flippancy: 'Should women think?' They gain in power perhaps, but do they not lose in happiness by thinking? If women must always labor under unjust economic conditions, receiving less pay for the same work than men, if women must always submit to the unjust social laws, based on the barbaric mosaic decree that the woman is to be stoned, and the man allowed to go free; if women must always see the children they have brought into the world with infinite pain and weariness, taken away from them to fight man-made battles over which no woman has any power; if women must always see their

sons degraded by man-made legislation and man-protected evils —
then I ask, Is it not a great mistake for women to think?

The Martha women, who fill their hands with labor and find their
highest delights in the day's work, are the happiest. That is, if these
things must always be, if we must always beat upon the bars of the
cage — we are foolish to beat; it is hard on the hands! Far better for
us to stop looking out and sit down and say: 'Good old cage — I
always did like a cage, anyway!'

But the question of whether or not women should think was
settled long ago. We must think because we were given something to
think with, ages ago, at the time of our creation. If God had not
intended us to think, he would not have given us our intelligence. It
would be a shabby trick, too, to give women brains to think, with no
hope of results, for thinking is just an aggravation if nothing comes
of it. It is a law of life that people will use what they have. That is
one theory of what caused the war. The nations were 'so good and
ready,' they just naturally fought. Mental activity is just as natural
for the woman peeling potatoes as it is for the man behind the plow,
and a little thinking will not hurt the quality of the work in either
case. There is in western Canada, one woman at least, who combines
thinking and working to great advantage. Her kitchen walls are hung
with mottoes and poems, which she commits to memory as she
works, and so while her hands are busy, she feeds her soul with the
bread of life.

The world has never been partial to the thinking woman — the
wise ones have always foreseen danger. Long years ago, when women
asked for an education, the world cried out that it would never do.
If women learned to read it would distract them from the real
business of life which was to make home happy for some good man.
If women learned to read there seemed to be a possibility that some
day some good man might come home and find his wife reading, and
the dinner not ready — and nothing could be imagined more horrible
than that! That seems to be the haunting fear of mankind — that the
advancement of women will sometime, someway, someplace, interfere with some man's comfort. There are many people who believe
that the physical needs of her family are a woman's only care; and
that strict attention to her husband's wardrobe and meals will insure
a happy marriage. Hand-embroidered slippers warmed and carefully
set out have ever been highly recommended as a potent charm to

hold masculine affection. They forget that men and children are not only food-eating and clothes-wearing animals — they are human beings with other and even greater needs than food and raiment.

Any person who believes that the average man marries the woman of his choice just because he wants a housekeeper and a cook, appraises mankind lower than I do. Intelligence on the wife's part does not destroy connubial bliss, neither does ignorance nor apathy ever make for it. Ideas do not break up homes, but lack of ideas. The light and airy silly fairy may get along beautifully in the days of courtship, but she palls a bit in the steady wear and tear of married life.

There was a picture in one of the popular woman's papers sometime ago, which taught a significant lesson. It was a breakfast scene. The young wife, daintily frilled in pink, sat at her end of the table in very apparent ill-humor — the young husband, quite unconscious of her, read the morning paper with evident interest. Below the picture there was a sharp criticism of the young man's neglect of his pretty wife and her dainty gown. Personally I sympathize with the young man and believe it would be a happier home if she were as interested in the paper as he and were reading the other half of it instead of sitting around feeling hurt.

But you see it is hard on the woman, just the same. All our civilization has taught her that pink frills were the thing. When they fail — she feels the bottom has dropped out of the world — he does not love her any more and she will go back to mother! You see the woman suffers every time.

Sometime we will teach our daughters that marriage is a divine partnership based on mutual love and community of interest, that sex attraction augmented by pink frills is only one part of it and not the most important; that the pleasant glowing embers of comradeship and loving friendship give out a warmer, more lasting, and more comfortable heat than the leaping flames of passion, and the happiest marriage is the one where the husband and wife come to regard each other as the dearest friend, the most congenial companion.

Women must think if they are going to make good in life; and success in marriage depends not alone on being good, but on making good! Men by their occupation are brought in contact with the world of ideas and affairs. They have been encouraged to be intelligent. Women have been encouraged to be foolish, and later on punished for the same foolishness, which is hardly fair.

But women are beginning to learn. Women are helping each other to see. They are coming together in clubs and societies and by this intercourse they are gaining a philosophy of life, which is helping them over the rough places of life. Most of us can get along very well on bright days, and when the going is easy, but we need something to keep us steady when the pathway is rough, and our wandering feet are in danger of losing their way. The most deadly uninteresting person, and the one who has the greatest temptation not to think at all, is the comfortable and happily married woman — the woman who has a good man between her and the world, who has not the saving privilege of having to work. A sort of fatty degeneration of the conscience sets in that is disastrous to the development of thought.

If women could be made to think, they would not wear immodest clothes, which suggest evil thoughts and awaken unlawful desires. If women could be made to think, they would see that it is woman's place to lift high the standard of morality. If women would only think, they would not wear aigrets and bird plumage which has caused the death of God's innocent and beautiful creatures. If women could be made to think, they would be merciful. If women would only think, they would not serve liquor to their guests, in the name of hospitality, and thus contribute to the degradation of mankind, and perhaps start some young man on the slippery way to ruin. If women would think about it, they would see that some mother, old and heartbroken, sitting up waiting for the staggering footsteps of her boy, might in her loneliness and grief and trouble curse the white hands that gave her lad his first drink. Women make life hard for other women because they do not think. And thinking seems to come hardest to the comfortable woman. A woman told me candidly and honestly not long ago that she was too comfortable to be interested in other people, and I have admired her for the truthfulness; she had diagnosed her own case accurately, and she did not babble of woman's sphere being her own home — she frankly admitted that she was selfish, and her comfort had caused it. I believe God intended us all to be happy and comfortable, clothed, fed, and housed, and there is no sin in comfort, unless we let it atrophy our souls, and settle down upon us like a stupor. Then it becomes a sin which destroys us. Let us pray:

From plague, pestilence and famine,
from battle, murder, sudden death,
and all forms of cowlike contentment,
 Good Lord, deliver us!

Chapter 5

The new chivalry

Brave women and fair men!

THIS seems to be a good time for us to jar ourselves lose from some of the prejudices and beliefs which we have outgrown. It is time for readjustment surely, a time for spiritual and mental housecleaning, when we are justified in looking things over very carefully and deciding whether or not we shall ever need them again.

Some of us have suspected for a long time that a good deal of the teaching of the world regarding women has come under the general heading of 'dope.' Now 'dope' is not a slang word, as you may be thinking, gentle reader. It is a good Anglo-Saxon word (or will be), for it fills a real need, and there is none other to take its place. 'Dope' means anything that is calculated to soothe, or hush, or put to sleep. 'Sedative' is a synonym, but it lacks the oily softness of 'dope.'

One of the commonest forms of dope given to women to keep them quiet is the one referred to in a previous chapter: 'The hand that rocks the cradle rules the world.' It is a great favorite with politicians and not being original with them it does contain a small element of truth. They use it in their pre-election speeches, which they begin with the honeyed words: 'We are glad to see we have with us this evening so many members of the fair sex; we are delighted to see that so many have come to grace our gathering on this occasion; we realize that a woman's intuition is ofttimes truer than a man's reasoning, and although women have no actual voice in politics, they have something far more strong and potent — they have the wonder power of indirect influence.' Just about here comes in 'the hand that rocks!'

Having thus administered the dope, in this pleasing mixture of molasses and soft soap, which is supposed to keep the 'fair sex' quiet and happy for the balance of the evening, the aspirant for public honors passes on to the serious business of the hour, and discusses the affairs of state with the electorate. Right here, let us sound a small note of warning. Keep your eye on the man who refers to women as the 'fair sex' — he is a dealer in dope!

One of the oldest and falsest of our beliefs regarding women is that they are protected — that some way in the battle of life they get the best of it. People talk of men's chivalry, that vague, indefinite quality which is supposed to transmute the common clay of life into gold.

Chivalry is a magic word. It seems to breathe of foreign strands and moonlight groves and silver sands and knights and earls and kings; it seems to tell of glorious deeds and waving plumes and prancing steeds and belted earls — and things!

People tell us of the good old days of chivalry when womanhood was really respected and reverenced — when brave knight rode gaily forth to die for his lady love. But in order to be really loved and respected there was one hard and fast condition laid down, to which all women must conform — they must be beautiful, no getting out of that. They simply had to have starry eyes and golden hair, or else black as a raven's wing; they had to have pale, white, and haughty brow, and a laugh like a ripple of magic. Then they were all right and armored knights would die for them quick as wink!

The homely women were all witches, dreadful witches, and they drowned them, on public holidays, in the mill pond!

People tell us now that chivalry is dead, and women have killed it, bold women who instead of staying at home, broidering pearls on a red velvet sleeve, have gone out to work — have gone to college side by side with men and have been so unwomanly sometimes as to take the prizes away from men. Chivalry cannot live in such an atmosphere. Certainly not!

Of course women can hardly be blamed for going out and working when one remembers that they must either work or starve. Broidering pearls will not boil the kettle worth a cent! There are now thirty per cent of the women of the U.S.A. and Canada, who are wage-earners, and we will readily grant that necessity has driven most of them out of their homes. Similarly, in England alone, there are a million and a half more women than men. It would seem that all women cannot have homes of their own — there does not seem to be enough men to go around. But still there are people who tell us these women should all have homes of their own — it is their own fault if they haven't; and once I heard of a woman saying the hardest thing about men I ever heard — and she was an ardent anti-suffragist too. She said that what was wrong with the women in England was that they were too particular — that's why they were not married, 'and,' she went on, 'any person can tell, when they look around at men in general, that God never intended women to be very particular.' I am glad I never said anything as hard as that about men.

There are still with us some of the conventions of the old days of chivalry. The pretty woman still has the advantage over her plainer sister — and the opinion of the world is that women must be beautiful at all costs. When a newspaper wishes to disprove a woman's contention, or demolish her theories, it draws ugly pictures of her. If it can show that she has big feet or red hands, or wears unbecoming clothes, that certainly settles the case — and puts her where she belongs.

This cruel convention that women must be beautiful accounts for the popularity of face-washes, and beauty parlors, and the languor of university extension lectures. Women cannot be blamed for this. All our civilization has been to the end that women make themselves attractive to men. The attractive woman has hitherto been the successful woman. The pretty girl marries a millionaire, travels in Europe, and is presented at court; her plainer sister, equally intelligent, marries a boy from home, and does her own washing. I am not comparing the two destinies as to which offers the greater opportunities for happiness or usefulness, but rather to show how widely divergent two lives may be. What caused the difference was a wavy strand of hair, a rounder curve on a cheek. Is it any wonder that women capitalize their good looks, even at the expense of their intelligence? The economic dependence of women is perhaps the greatest injustice that has been done to us, and has worked the greatest injury to the race.

Men are not entirely blameless in respect to the frivolity of women. It is easy to blame women for dressing foolishly, extravagantly, but to what end do they do it? To be attractive to men; and the reason they continue to do it is that it is successful. Many a woman has found that it pays to be foolish. Men like frivolity — before marriage; but they demand all the sterner virtues afterwards. The little dainty, fuzzy-haired, simpering dolly who chatters and wears toe-slippers has a better chance in the matrimonial market than the clear-headed, plainer girl, who dresses sensibly. A little boy once gave his mother directions as to his birthday present — he said he wanted 'something foolish' and therein he expressed a purely masculine wish.

A man's ideal at seventeen
   Must be a sprite —
A dainty, fairy, elfish queen
   Of pure delight;
But later on he sort of feels
He'd like a girl who could cook meals.

Life is full of anomalies, and in the mating and pairing of men and women there are many.

Why is the careless, easy-going, irresponsible way of the young girl so attractive to men? It does not make for domestic happiness; and why, Oh why, do some of our best men marry such odd little sticks of pin-head women, with a brain similar in caliber to a second-rate butterfly, while the most intelligent, unselfish, and womanly women are left unmated? I am going to ask about this the first morning I am in heaven, if so be we are allowed to ask about the things which troubled us while on our mortal journey. I have never been able to find out about it here.

Now this old belief that women are protected is of sturdy growth and returns to life with great persistence. Theoretically women are protected – on paper – traditionally – just like Belgium was, and with just as disastrous results.

A member of the English Parliament declared with great emphasis that the women now have everything the heart could desire – they reign like queens and can have their smallest wish gratified. ('Smallest' is right.) And we very readily grant that there are many women living in idleness and luxury on the bounty of their male relatives, and we say it with sorrow and shame that these are estimated the successful women in the opinion of the world. But while some feast in idleness, many others slave in poverty. The great army of women workers are ill-paid, badly housed, and their work is not honored or respected or paid for. What share have they in man's chivalry? Chivalry is like a line of credit. You can get plenty of it when you do not need it. When you are prospering financially and your bank account is growing and you are rated A1, you can get plenty of credit – it is offered to you; but when the dark days of financial depression overtake you, and the people you are depending upon do not 'come through,' and you must have credit – must have it! – the very people who once urged it upon you will now tell you that 'money is tight!'

The young and pretty woman, well dressed and attractive, can get all the chivalry she wants. She will have seats offered her on street cars, men will hasten to carry her parcels, or open doors for her; but the poor old woman, beaten in the battle of life, sick of life's struggles, and grown gray and weather-beaten facing life's storms – what chivalry is shown her? She can go her weary way uncomforted and unattended. People who need it do not get it.

Anyway, chivalry is a poor substitute for justice, if one cannot have both. Chivalry is something like the icing on the cake, sweet but not nourishing. It is like the paper lace around the bonbon box – we could get along without it.

There are countless thousands of truly chivalrous men, who have the true chivalry whose foundation is justice – who would protect all women from injury of insult or injustice, but who know that they cannot do it – who know that in spite of all they can do, women are often outraged, insulted, ill-treated. The truly chivalrous man, who does reverence all womankind, realizing this, says: 'Let us give women every weapon whereby they can defend themselves; let us remove the stigma of political nonentity under which women have been placed. Let us give women a fair deal!'

This is the new chivalry – and on it we build our hope.

Chapter 6

Hardy perennials!

I hold it true — I will not change,
   For changes are a dreadful bore —
That nothing must be done on earth
   Unless it has been done before.
Anti-Suffrage Creed

IF PREJUDICES belonged to the vegetable world they would be described under the general heading of: 'Hardy Perennials; will grow in any soil, and bloom without ceasing; requiring no cultivation; will do better when left alone.'

In regard to tenacity of life, no old yellow cat has anything on a prejudice. You may kill it with your own hands, bury it deep, and sit on the grave, and behold! the next day, it will walk in at the back door, purring.

Take some of the prejudices regarding women that have been exploded and blown to pieces many, many times and yet walk among us today in the fulness of life and vigor. There is a belief that housekeeping is the only occupation for women; that all women must be housekeepers, whether they like it or not. Men may do as they like, and indulge their individuality, but every true and womanly woman must take to the nutmeg grater and the O-Cedar Mop. It is also believed that in the good old days before woman suffrage was discussed, and when woman's clubs were unheard of, that all women adored housework, and simply pined for Monday morning to come to get at the weekly wash; that women cleaned house with rapture and cooked joyously. Yet there is a story told of one of the women of the old days, who arose at four o'clock in the morning, and aroused all her family at an indecently early hour for breakfast, her reason being that she wanted to get 'one of these horrid old meals over.' This woman had never been at a suffrage meeting — so where did she get the germ of discontent?

At the present time there is much discontent among women, and many people are seriously alarmed about it. They say women are no longer contented with woman's sphere and woman's work — that the washboard has lost its charm, and the days of the hair-wreath are ended. We may as well admit that there is discontent among women. We cannot drive them back to the spinning wheel and the mathook, for they will not go. But there is really no cause for alarm, for discontent is not necessarily wicked. There is such a thing as divine discontent just as there is criminal contentment. Discontent may mean the stirring of ambition, the desire to spread out, to improve and grow. Discontent is a sign of life, corresponding to growing pains in a healthy child. The poor woman who is making a brave struggle for existence is not saying much, though she is thinking all the time. In the old days when a woman's hours were from 5 A.M. to 5 A.M., we did not hear much of discontent among women, because they had not time to even talk, and certainly could not get together. The horse on the treadmill may be very discontented, but he is not disposed to tell his troubles, for he cannot stop to talk.

It is the women, who now have leisure, who are doing the talking. For generations women have been thinking and thought without expression is dynamic, and gathers volume by repression. Evolution when blocked and suppressed becomes revolution. The introduction of machinery and the factory-made articles has given women more leisure than they had formerly, and now the question arises, what are they going to do with it?

Custom and conventionality recommend many and varied occupations for women, social functions intermixed with kindly deeds of charity, embroidering altar cloths, making strong and durable garments for the poor, visiting the sick, comforting the sad, all of which women have faithfully done, but while they have been doing these things, they have been wondering about the underlying causes of poverty, sadness and sin. They notice that when the unemployed are fed on Christmas day, they are just as hungry as ever on December the twenty-sixth, or at least on December the twenty-seventh; they have been led to inquire into the causes for little children being left in the care of the state, and they find that in over half of the cases, the liquor traffic has contributed to the poverty and unworthiness of the parents. The state which licenses the traffic steps in and takes care, or tries to, of the victims; the rich brewer whose business it is to encourage drinking, is usually the largest giver to the work of the Children's Aid Society, and is often extolled for his lavish generosity: and sometimes when women think about these things they are struck by the absurdity of a system which allows one man or a body of men to rob a child of his father's love and care all year, and then gives him a stuffed dog and a little red sleigh at Christmas and calls it charity!

Women have always done their share of the charity work of the world. The lady of the manor, in the old feudal days, made warm mittens and woolen mufflers with her own white hands and carried them to the cottages at Christmas, along with blankets and coals. And it was a splendid arrangement all through, for it furnished the lady with mild and pleasant occupation, and it helped to soothe the conscience of the lord, and if the cottagers (who were often 'low worthless fellows, much given up to riotous thinking and disputing') were disposed to wonder why they had to work all year and get nothing, while the lord of the manor did nothing all year and got everything, the gift of blanket and coals, the warm mufflers, and 'a shawl for granny' showed them what ungrateful souls they were.

Women have dispensed charity for many, many years, but gradually it has dawned upon them that the most of our charity is very ineffectual, and merely smoothes things over, without ever reaching the root. A great deal of our charity is like the kindly deed of the benevolent old gentleman, who found a sick dog by the wayside, lying in the full glare of a scorching sun. The tender-hearted old man climbed down from his carriage, and, lifting the dog tenderly in his arms, carried him around into the small patch of shade cast by his carriage.

'Lie there, my poor fellow!' he said. 'Lie there, in the cool shade, where the sun's rays may not smite you!'

Then he got into his carriage and drove away.

Women have been led, through their charitable institutions and philanthropic endeavors, to do some thinking about causes.

Mrs. B. set out to be a 'family friend' to the family of her washwoman. Mrs. B. was a thoroughly charitable, kindly disposed woman, who had never favored woman's suffrage and regarded the new movement among women with suspicion. Her washwoman's family consisted of four children, and a husband who blew in gaily once in a while when in need of funds, or when recovering from a protracted spree, which made a few days' nursing very welcome. His wife, a Polish woman, had the old-world reverence for men, and obeyed him implicitly; she still felt it was very sweet of him to come home at all. Mrs. B. had often declared that Polly's devotion to her husband was a beautiful thing to see. The two eldest boys had newspaper routes and turned in their earnings regularly, and, although the husband did not contribute anything but his occasional company, Polly was able to make the payments on their little four-roomed cottage. In another year, it would be all paid for.

But one day Polly's husband began to look into the law — as all men should — and he saw that he had been living far below his privileges. The cottage was his — not that he had ever paid a cent on it, of course, but his wife had, and she was his; and the cottage was in his name.

So he sold it; naturally he did not consult Polly, for he was a quiet, peaceful man, and not fond of scenes. So he sold it quietly, and with equal quietness he withdrew from the Province, and took the money with him. He did not even say good-by to Polly or the children, which was rather ungrateful, for they had given him many a meal and night's lodging. When Polly came crying one Monday morning and told her story, Mrs. B. could not believe it, and assured Polly she must be mistaken, but Polly declared that a man had come and asked her did she wish to rent the house for he had bought it. Mrs. B. went at once to the lawyers who had completed the deal. They were a reputable firm and Mrs. B. knew one of the partners quite well. She was sure Polly's husband could not sell the cottage. But the lawyers assured her it was quite true. They were very gentle and patient with Mrs. B. and listened courteously to her explanation, and did not dispute her word at all when she explained that Polly and her two boys had paid every cent on the house. It seemed that a trifling little thing like that did not matter. It did not really matter who paid for the house; the husband was the owner, for was he not the head of the house? and the property was in his name.

Polly was graciously allowed to rent her own cottage for $12.50 a month, with an option of buying, and the two little boys are still on a morning route delivering one of the city dailies.

Mrs. B. has joined a suffrage society and makes speeches on the injustice of the laws; and yet she began innocently enough, by making strong and durable garments for her washwoman's children — and see what has come of it! If women would only be content to snip away at the symptoms of poverty and distress, feeding the hungry and clothing the naked, all would be well and they would be much commended for their kindness of heart; but when they begin to inquire into causes, they find themselves in the sacred realm of politics where prejudice says no women must enter.

A woman may take an interest in factory girls, and hold meetings for them, and encourage them to walk in virtue's ways all she likes, but if she begins to advocate more sanitary surroundings for them, with some respect for the common decencies of life, she will find herself again in that sacred realm of politics — confronted by a factory act, on which no profane female hand must be laid.

Now politics simply means public affairs — yours and mine, everybody's — and to say that politics are too corrupt for women is a weak and foolish statement for any man to make. Any man who is actively engaged in politics, and declares that politics are too corrupt for women, admits one of two things, either that he is a party to this corruption, or that he is unable to prevent it — and in either case something should be done. Politics are not inherently vicious. The office of lawmaker should be the highest in the land, equaled in honor only by that of the minister of the gospel. In the old days, the two were combined with very good effect; but they seem to have drifted apart in more recent years.

If politics are too corrupt for women, they are too corrupt for men; for men and women are one — indissolubly joined together for good or ill. Many men have tried to put all their religion and virtue in their wife's name, but it does not work very well. When social conditions are corrupt women cannot escape by shutting their eyes, and taking no interest. It would be far better to give them a chance to clean them up.

What would you think of a man who would say to his wife: 'This house to which I am bringing you to live is very dirty and unsanitary, but I will not allow you — the dear wife whom I have sworn to protect — to touch it. It is too dirty for your precious little white hands! You must stay upstairs, dear. Of course the odor from below may come up to you, but use your smelling salts and think no evil. I do not hope to ever be able to clean it up, but certainly you must never think of trying.'

Do you think any woman would stand for that? She would say: 'John, you are all right in your way, but there are some places where your brain skids. Perhaps you had better stay downtown today for lunch. But on your way down please call at the grocer's, and send me a scrubbing brush and a package of Dutch Cleanser, and some chloride of lime, and now hurry.' Women have cleaned up things since time began; and if women ever get into politics there will be a cleaning-out of pigeon-holes and forgotten corners, on which the dust of years has fallen, and the sound of the political carpet-beater will be heard in the land.

There is another hardy perennial that constantly lifts its head above the earth, persistently refusing to be ploughed under, and that is that if women were ever given a chance to participate in outside affairs, that family quarrels would result; that men and their wives who have traveled the way of life together, side by side for years, and come safely through religious discussions, and discussions relating to 'his' people and 'her' people, would angrily rend each other over politics, and great damage to the furniture would be the result. Father and son have been known to live under the same roof and vote differently, and yet live! Not only to live, but live peaceably! If a husband and wife are going to quarrel they will find a cause for dispute easily enough, and will not be compelled to wait for election day. And supposing that they have never, never had a single dispute, and not a ripple has ever marred the placid surface of their matrimonial sea, I believe that a small family jar — or at least a real lively argument — will do them good. It is in order to keep the white-winged angel of peace hovering over the home that married women are not allowed to vote in many places. Spinsters and widows are counted worthy of voice in the selection of school trustee, and alderman, and mayor, but not the woman who has taken to herself a husband and still has him.

What a strange commentary on marriage that it should disqualify a woman from voting. Why should marriage disqualify a woman? Men have been known to vote for years after they were dead!

Quite different from the 'family jar' theory, another reason is advanced against married women voting — it is said that they would all vote with their husbands, and that the married man's vote would thereby be doubled. We believe it is eminently right and proper that husband and wife should vote the same way, and in that case no one would be able to tell whether the wife was voting with the husband or the husband voting with the wife. Neither would it matter. If giving the franchise to women did nothing more than double the married man's vote it would do a splendid thing for the country, for the married man is the best voter we have; generally speaking, he is a man of family and property — surely if we can depend on anyone we can depend upon him, and if by giving his wife a vote we can double his — we have done something to offset the irresponsible transient vote of the man who has no interest in the community.

There is another sturdy prejudice that blooms everywhere in all climates, and that is that women would not vote if they had the privilege; and this is many times used as a crushing argument against woman suffrage. But why worry? If women do not use it, then surely there is no harm done; but those who use the argument seem to imply that a vote unused is a very dangerous thing to leave lying around, and will probably spoil and blow up. In support of this statement instances are cited of women letting their vote lie idle and unimproved in elections for school trustee and alderman. Of course, the percentage of men voting in these contests was quite small, too, but no person finds fault with that.

Women may have been careless about their franchise in elections where no great issue is at stake, but when moral matters are being decided women have not shown any lack of interest. As a result of the first vote cast by the women of Illinois over one thousand saloons went out of business. Ask the liquor dealers if they think women will use the ballot. They do not object to woman suffrage on the ground that women will not vote, but because they will.

'Why, Uncle Henry!' exclaimed one man to another on election day. 'I never saw you out to vote before. What struck you?'

'Hadn't voted for fifteen years,' declared Uncle Henry, 'but you bet I came out today to vote against givin' these fool women a vote; what's the good of givin' them a vote? they wouldn't use it!'

Then, of course, on the other hand there are those who claim that women would vote too much — that they would vote not wisely but too well; that they would take up voting as a life work to the exclusion of husband, home and children. There seems to be considerable misapprehension on the subject of voting. It is really a simple and perfectly innocent performance, quickly over, and with no bad after-effects.

It is usually done in a vacant room in a school or the vestry of a church, or a town hall. No drunken men stare at you. You are not jostled or pushed — you wait your turn in an orderly line, much as you have waited to buy a ticket at a railway station. Two tame and quiet-looking men sit at a table, and when your turn comes, they ask you your name, which is perhaps slightly embarrassing, but it is not as bad as it might be, for they do not ask your age, or of what disease did your grandmother die. You go behind the screen with your ballot paper in your hand, and there you find a seal-brown pencil tied with a chaste white string. Even the temptation of annexing the pencil is removed from your frail humanity. You mark your ballot, and drop it in the box, and come out into the sunlight again. If you had never heard that you had done an unladylike thing you would not know it. It all felt solemn, and serious, and very respectable to you, something like a Sunday-school convention.

Then, too, you are surprised at what a short time you have been away from home. You put the potatoes on when you left home, and now you are back in time to strain them.

In spite of the testimony of many reputable women that they have been able to vote and get the dinner on one and the same day, there still exists a strong belief that the whole household machinery goes out of order when a woman goes to vote. No person denies a woman the right to go to church, and yet the church service takes a great deal more time than voting. People even concede to women the right to go shopping, or visiting a friend, or an occasional concert. But the wife and mother, with her God-given, sacred trust of molding the young life of our land, must never dream of going round the corner to vote. 'Who will mind the baby?' cried one of our public men, in great agony of spirit, 'when the mother goes to vote?'

One woman replied that she thought she could get the person that minded it when she went to pay her taxes — which seemed to be a fairly reasonable proposition. Yet the hardy plant of prejudice flourishes, and the funny pictures still bring a laugh.

Father comes home, tired, weary, footsore, toe-nails ingrowing, caused by undarned stockings, and finds the fire out, house cold and empty, save for his half-dozen children, all crying.

'Where is your mother?' the poor man asks in broken tones. For a moment the sobs are hushed while little Ellie replies: 'Out voting!'

Father bursts into tears.

Of course, people tell us, it is not the mere act of voting which demoralizes women — if they would only vote and be done with it; but women are creatures of habit, and habits once formed are hard to break; and although the polls are only open every three or four years, if women once get into the way of going to them, they will hang around there all the rest of the time. It is in woman's impressionable nature that the real danger lies.

Another shoot of this hardy shrub of prejudice is that women are too good to mingle in everyday life — they are too sweet and too frail — that women are angels. If women are angels we should try to get them into public life as soon as possible, for there is a great shortage of angels there just at present, if all we hear is true.

Then there is the pedestal theory — that women are away up on a pedestal, and down below, looking up at them with deep adoration, are men, their willing slaves. Sitting up on a pedestal does not appeal very strongly to a healthy woman – and, besides, if a woman has been on a pedestal for any length of time, it must be very hard to have to come down and cut the wood.

These tender-hearted and chivalrous gentlemen who tell you of their adoration for women, cannot bear to think of women occupying public positions. Their tender hearts shrink from the idea of women lawyers or women policemen, or even women preachers; these positions would 'rub the bloom off the peach,' to use their own eloquent words. They cannot bear, they say, to see women leaving the sacred precincts of home – and yet their offices are scrubbed by women who do their work while other people sleep – poor women who leave the sacred precincts of home to earn enough to keep the breath of life in them, who carry their scrub-pails home, through the deserted streets, long after the cars have stopped running. They are exposed to cold, to hunger, to insult – poor souls – is there any pity felt for them? Not that we have heard of. The tender-hearted ones can bear this with equanimity. It is the thought of women getting into comfortable and well-paid positions which wrings their manly hearts.

Another aspect of the case is that women can do more with their indirect influence than by the ballot; though just why they cannot do better still with both does not appear to be very plain. The ballot is a straight-forward dignified way of making your desire or choice felt. There are some things which are not pleasant to talk about, but would be delightful to vote against. Instead of having to beg, and coax, and entreat, and beseech, and denounce as women have had to do all down the centuries, in regard to the evil things which threaten to destroy their homes and those whom they love, what a glorious thing it would be if women could go out and vote against these things. It seems like a straightforward and easy way of expressing one's opinion.

But, of course, popular opinion says it is not 'womanly.' The 'womanly way' is to nag and tease. Women have often been told that if they go about it right they can get anything. They are encouraged to plot and scheme, and deceive, and wheedle, and coax for things. This is womanly and sweet. Of course, if this fails, they still have tears – they can always cry and have hysterics, and raise hob generally, but they must do it in a womanly way. Will the time ever come when the word 'feminine' will have in it no trace of trickery?

Women are too sentimental to vote, say the politicians sometimes. Sentiment is nothing to be ashamed of, and perhaps an
infusion of sentiment in politics is what we need. Honor and
honesty, love and loyalty, are only sentiments, and yet they make
the fabric out of which our finest traditions are woven. The United
States has sent carloads of flour to starving Belgium because of a
sentiment. Belgium refused to let Germany march over her land
because of a sentiment, and Canada has responded to the SOS call of
the Empire because of a sentiment. It seems that it is sentiment
which redeems our lives from sordidness and selfishness, and
occasionally gives us a glimpse of the upper country.

For too long people have regarded politics as a scheme whereby
easy money might be obtained. Politics has meant favors, pulls, easy
jobs for friends, new telephone lines, ditches. The question has not
been: 'What can I do for my country?' but: 'What can I get? What is
there in this for me?' The test of a member of Parliament as voiced
by his constitutents has been: 'What has he got for us?' The good
member who will be elected the next time is the one who did not
forget his friends, who got us a Normal School, or a Court House, or
an Institution for the Blind, something that we could see or touch,
eat or drink. Surely a touch of sentiment in politics would do no
harm.

Then there is the problem of the foreign woman's vote. Many
people fear that the granting of woman suffrage would greatly
increase the unintelligent vote, because the foreign women would
then have the franchise, and in our blind egotism we class our
foreign people as ignorant people, if they do not know our ways and
our language. They may know many other languages, but if they
have not yet mastered ours they are poor, ignorant foreigners. We
Anglo-Saxon people have a decided sense of our own superiority,
and we feel sure that our skin is exactly the right color, and we
people from Huron and Bruce feel sure that we were born in the
right place, too. So we naturally look down upon those who happen
to be of a different race and tongue than our own.

It is a sad feature of humanity that we are disposed to hate what
we do not understand; we naturally suspect and distrust where we
do not know. Hens are like that, too! When a strange fowl comes
into a farmyard all the hens take a pick at it — not that it has done
anything wrong, but they just naturally do not like the look of its

face because it is strange. Now that may be very good ethics for hens, but it is hardly good enough for human beings. Our attitude toward the foreign people was well exemplified in one of the missions, where a little Italian boy, who had been out two years, refused to sit beside a newly arrived Italian boy, who, of course, could not speak a word of English. The teacher asked him to sit with his lately arrived compatriot, so that he might interpret for him. The older boy flatly refused, and told the teacher he 'had no use for them young dagos.'

'You see,' said the teacher sadly, when telling the story, 'he had caught the Canadian spirit.'

People say hard things about the corruptible foreign vote, but they place the emphasis in the wrong place. Instead of using our harsh adjectives for the poor fellow who sells his vote, let us save them all for the corrupt politician who buys it, for he cannot plead ignorance – he knows what he is doing. The foreign people who come to Canada, come with burning enthusiasm for the new land, this land of liberty – land of freedom. Some have been seen kissing the ground in an ecstacy of gladness when they arrive. It is the land of their dreams, where they hope to find home and happiness. They come to us with ideals of citizenship that shame our narrow, mercenary standards. These men are of a race which has gladly shed its blood for freedom and is doing it today. But what happens? They go out to work on construction gangs for the summer, they earn money for several months, and when the work closes down they drift back into the cities. They have done the work we wanted them to do, and no further thought is given to them. They may get off the earth so far as we are concerned. One door stands invitingly open to them. There is one place they are welcome – so long as their money lasts – and around the bar they get their ideals of citizenship.

When an election is held, all at once this new land of their adoption begins to take an interest in them, and political heelers, well paid for the job, well armed with whiskey, cigars and money, go among them, and, in their own language, tell them which way they must vote – and they do. Many an election has been swung by this means. One new arrival, just learning our language, expressed his contempt for us by exclaiming: 'Bah! Canada is not a country – it's just a place to make money.' That was all he had seen. He spoke correctly from his point of view.

Then when the elections are over, and the Government is sustained, the men who have climbed back to power by these means speak eloquently of our 'foreign people who have come to our shores to find freedom under the sheltering folds of our grand old flag (cheers), on which the sun never sets, and under whose protection all men are free and equal – with an equal chance of molding the destiny of the great Empire of which we make a part.' (Cheers and prolonged applause.)

If we really understood how, with our low political ideals and iniquitous election methods, we have corrupted the souls of these men who have come to live among us, we would no longer cheer, when we hear this old drivel of the 'folds of the flag.' We would think with shame of how we have driven the patriotism out of these men and replaced it by the greed of gain, and instead of cheers and applause we would cry: 'Lord, have mercy upon us!'

The foreign women, whom politicians and others look upon as such a menace, are differently dealt with than the men. They do not go out to work, *en masse,* as the men do. They work one by one, and are brought in close contact with their employers. The women who go out washing and cleaning spend probably five days a week in the homes of other women. Surely one of her five employers will take an interest in her, and endeavor to instruct her in the duties of citizenship. Then, too, the mission work is nearly all done for women and girls. The foreign women generally speak English before the men, for the reason that they are brought in closer contact with English-speaking people. When I hear people speaking of the ignorant foreign women I think of 'Mary,' and 'Annie,' and others I have known. I see their broad foreheads and intelligent kindly faces, and think of the heroic struggle they are making to bring their families up in thrift and decency. Would Mary vote against liquor if she had the chance? She would. So would you if your eyes had been blackened as often by a drunken husband. There is no need to instruct these women on the evils of liquor drinking – they are able to give you a few aspects of the case which perhaps you had not thought of. We have no reason to be afraid of the foreign woman's vote. I wish we were as sure of the ladies who live on the Avenue.

There are people who tell us that the reason women must never be allowed to vote is because they do not want to vote, the inference being that women are never given anything that they do not want. It sounds so chivalrous and protective and high-minded. But women have always got things that they did not want. Women do not want the liquor business, but they have it; women do not want less pay for the same work as men, but they get it. Women did not want the present war, but they have it. The fact of women's preference has never been taken very seriously, but it serves here just as well as anything else. Even the opponents of woman suffrage will admit that some women want to vote, but they say they are a very small minority, and 'not our best women.' That is a classification which is rather difficult of proof and of no importance anyway. It does not matter whether it is the best, or second best, or the worst who are asking for a share in citizenship; voting is not based on morality, but on humanity. No man votes because he is one of our best men. He votes because he is of the male sex, and over twenty-one years of age. The fact that many women are indifferent on the subject does not alter the situation. People are indifferent about many things that they should be interested in. The indifference of people on the subject of ventilation and hygiene does not change the laws of health. The indifference of many parents on the subject of an education for their children does not alter the value of education. If one woman wants to vote, she should have that opportunity just as if one woman desires a college education, she should not be held back because of the indifferent careless ones who do not desire it. Why should the mentally inert, careless, uninterested woman, who cares nothing for humanity but is contented to patter along her own little narrow way, set the pace for the others of us? Voting will not be compulsory; the shrinking violets will not be torn from their shady fence-corner; the 'home bodies' will be able to still sit in rapt contemplation of their own fireside. We will not force the vote upon them, but why should they force their votelessness upon us?

'My wife does not want to vote,' declared one of our Canadian premiers in reply to a delegation of women who asked for the vote. 'My wife would not vote if she had the chance,' he further stated. No person had asked about his wife, either.

'I will not have my wife sit in Parliament,' another man cried in alarm, when he was asked to sign a petition giving women full right of franchise. We tried to soothe his fears. We delicately and tactfully declared that his wife was safe. She would not be asked to go to Parliament by any of us — we gave him our word that she was immune from public duties of that nature, for we knew the lady and her limitations, and we knew she was safe — safe as a glass of milk at an old-fashioned logging-bee; safe as a dish of cold bread pudding at a strawberry festival. She would not have to leave home to serve her country at 'the earnest solicitation of friends' or otherwise. But he would not sign. He saw his 'Minnie' climbing the slippery ladder of political fame. It would be his Minnie who would be chosen — he felt it coming, the sacrifice would fall on his one little ewe-lamb.

After one has listened to all these arguments and has contracted clergyman's sore throat talking back, it is real relief to meet the people who say flatly and without reason: 'You can't have it — no — I won't argue — but inasmuch as I can prevent it — you will never vote! So there!' The men who meet the question like this are so easy to classify.

I remember when I was a little girl back on the farm in the Souris Valley, I used to water the cattle on Saturday mornings, drawing the water in an icy bucket with a windlass from a fairly deep well. We had one old white ox, called Mike, a patriarchal-looking old sinner, who never had enough, and who always had to be watered first. Usually I gave him what I thought he should have and then took him back to the stable and watered the others. But one day I was feeling real strong, and I resolved to give Mike all he could drink, even if it took every drop of water in the well. I must admit that I cherished a secret hope that he would kill himself drinking. I will not set down here in cold figures how many pails of water Mike drank — but I remember. At last he could not drink another drop, and stood shivering beside the trough, blowing the last mouthful out of his mouth like a bad child. I waited to see if he would die, or at least turn away and give the others a chance. The thirsty cattle came crowding around him, but old Mike, so full I am sure he felt he would never drink another drop of water again as long as he lived, deliberately and with difficulty put his two front feet over the trough and kept all the other cattle away ... Years afterwards I had the pleasure of being present when a delegation waited upon the Government of one of the provinces of Canada, and presented many reasons for extending the franchise to women. One member of the Government arose and spoke for all his colleagues. He said in substance: 'You can't have it — so long as I have anything to do with the affairs of this province — you shall not have it!' ...

Did your brain ever give a queer little twist, and suddenly you were conscious that the present mental process had taken place before. If you have ever had it, you will know what I mean, and if you haven't I cannot make you understand. I had that feeling then ... I said to myself: 'Where have I seen that face before?' ... Then, suddenly, I remembered, and in my heart I cried out: 'Mike! — old friend, Mike! Dead these many years! Your bones lie buried under the fertile soil of the Souris Valley, but your soul goes marching on! Mike, old friend, I see you again — both feet in the trough!'

Chapter 7

Gentle lady

The soul that idleth will surely die.

I AM sorry to have to say so, but there are some women who love to
be miserable, who have a perfect genius for martyrdom, who take a
delight in seeing how badly they can be treated, who seek out hard
ways for their feet, who court tears rather than laughter. Such a one
is hard to live with, for they glory in their cross, and simply revel in
their burdens, and they so contrive that all who come in contact
with them become a party to their martyrdom, and thus even
innocent people, who never intended to oppress the weak or harass
the innocent, are led into these heinous sins.

Mrs. M. was one of these. She prided herself on never telling
anyone to do what she could dc herself. Her own poetic words were:
'I'd crawl on my hands and knees before I would ask anyone to do
things for me. If they can't see what's to be done, I'll not tell them.'
This was her declaration of independence. Needless to say, Mrs. M.
had a large domestic help problem. Her domestic helpers were
continually going and coming. The inefficient ones she would not
keep, and the efficient ones would not stay with her. So the burden
of the home fell heavily on her, and, pulling her martyr's crown
close down on her head, she worked feverishly. When she was not
working she was bemoaning her sad lot, and indulging in large drafts
of self-pity. The holidays she spent were in sanatoriums and
hospitals, but she gloried in her illnesses.

She would make the journey upstairs for the scissors rather than
ask anyone to bring them down for her, and then cherish a hurt
feeling for the next hour because nobody noticed that she was
needing scissors. She expected all her family, and the maids
especially, to be mind readers, and because they were not she was
bitterly grieved. There is not much hope for people when they make
a virtue of their sins.

She often told the story of what happened when her Tommy was
two days old. She told it to illustrate her independence of character,
but most people thought it showed something quite different. Mr.
M. was displeased with his dinner on this particular day, and, in his
blundering man's way, complained to his wife about the cooking and
left the house without finishing his meal. Mrs. M. forthwith decided
that she would wear the martyr's crown again and some more! She
got up and cooked the next meal, in spite of the wild protests of the
frightened maid and nurse, who foresaw disaster. Mrs. M. took
violently ill as a result of her exertions just as she hoped she would,

and now, after a lapse of twenty years, proudly tells that her subsequent illness lasted six weeks and cost six hundred dollars, and she is proud of it!

A wiser woman would have handled the situation with tact. When Mr. M. came storming upstairs, waving his table-napkin and feeling much abused, she would have calmed him down by telling him not to wake the baby, thereby directing his attention to the small pink traveler who had so recently joined the company. She would have explained to him that even if his dinner had not been quite satisfactory, he was lucky to get anything in troublous times like these; she would have told him that if, having to eat poor meals was all the discomfiture that came his way, he was getting off light and easy. She might even go so far as to remind him that the one who asks the guests must always pay the piper.

There need not have been any heartburnings or regrets or perturbation of spirit. Mr. M. would have felt ashamed of his outbreak and apologized to her and to the untroubled Tommy, and gone downstairs, and eaten his stewed prunes with an humble and thankful heart.

This love of martyrdom is deeply ingrained in the heart of womankind, and comes from long bitter years of repression and tyranny. An old handbook on etiquette earnestly enjoins all young ladies who desire to be pleasing in the eyes of men to 'avoid a light rollicking manner, and to cultivate a sweet plaintiveness, as of hidden sorrow bravely borne.' It also declares that if any young lady has a robust frame, she must be careful to dissemble it, for it is in her frailty that woman can make her greatest appeal to man. No man wishes to marry an Amazon. It also earnestly commends a piece of sewing to be ever in the hand of the young lady who would attract the opposite sex! The use of large words or any show of learning or of unseemly intelligence is to be carefully avoided.

People have all down the centuries blocked out for women a weeping part. 'Man must work and women must weep.' So the habit of martyrdom has sort of settled down on us.

I will admit there has been some reason for it. Women do suffer more than men. They are physically smaller and weaker, more highly sensitive and therefore have a greater capacity for suffering. They have all the ordinary ills of humanity, and then some! They have above all been the victims of wrong thinking – they have been steeped in tears and false sentiments. People still speak of womanhood as if it were a disease.

Society has had its lash raised for women everywhere, and some have taken advantage of this to serve their own ends. An orphan girl, ignorant of the world's ways and terribly frightened of them, was told by her mistress that if she were to leave the roof which sheltered her she would get 'talked about,' and lose her good name. So she was able to keep the orphan working for five dollars a month. She used the lash to her own advantage.

Fear of 'talk' has kept many a woman quiet. Woman's virtue has been heavy responsibility not to be forgotten for an instant.

'Remember, Judge,' cried out a woman about to be sentenced for stealing, 'that I am an honest woman.'

'I believe you are,' replied the judge, 'and I will be lenient with you.'

The word 'honest' as applied to women means 'virtuous.' It has overshadowed all other virtues, and in a way appeared to make them of no account.

The physical disabilities of women which have been augmented and exaggerated by our insane way of dressing has had much to do with shaping women's thought. The absurdly tight skirts which prevented the wearer from walking like a human being, made a pitiful cry to the world. They were no doubt worn as a protest against the new movement among women, which has for its object the larger liberty, the larger humanity of women. The hideous mincing gait of the tightly-skirted women seems to speak. It said: 'I am not a useful human being — see! I cannot walk — I dare not run, but I am a woman — I still have my sex to commend me. I am not of use, I am made to be supported. My sex is my only appeal.'

Rather an indelicate and unpleasant thought, too, for an 'honest' woman to advertise so brazenly. The tight skirts and diaphanous garments were plainly a return to 'sex.' The ultra feminine felt they were going to lose something in this agitation for equality. They do not want rights — they want privileges — like the servants who prefer tips to wages. This is not surprising. Keepers of wild animals tell us that when an animal has been a long time in captivity it prefers captivity to freedom, and even when the door of the cage is opened it will not come out — but that is no argument against freedom.

The anti-suffrage attitude of mind is not so much a belief as a disease. I read a series of anti-suffrage articles not long ago in the

New York Times. They all were written in the same strain: 'We are gentle ladies. Protect us. We are weak, very weak, but very loving.' There was not one strong nourishing sentence that would inspire anyone to fight the good fight. It was all anemic and bloodless, and beseeching, and had the indefinable sick-headache, kimona, breakfast-in-bed quality in it, that repels the strong and healthy. They talked a great deal of the care and burden of motherhood. They had no gleam of humor — not one. The anti-suffragists dwell much on what a care children are. Their picture of a mother is a tired, faded, bedraggled woman, with a babe in her arms, two other small children holding to her skirts, all crying. According to them, children never grow up, and no person can ever attend to them but the mother. Of course, the anti-suffragists are not this kind themselves. Not at all. They talk of potential motherhood — but that is usually about as far as they go. Potential motherhood sounds well and hurts nobody.

The Gentle Lady still believes in the masculine terror of tears, and the judicious use of fainting. The Jane Austen heroine always did it and it worked well. She burst into tears on one page and fainted dead away on the next. That just showed what a gentle lady she was, and what a tender heart she had, and it usually did the trick. Lord Algernon was there to catch her in his arms. She would not faint if he wasn't.

The Gentle Lady does not like to hear distressing things. Said a very gentle lady not long ago: 'Now, please do not tell me about how these ready-to-wear garments are made, because I do not wish to know. The last time I heard a woman talk about the temptation of factory girls, my head ached all evening and I could not sleep.' (When the Gentle Lady has a headache it is no small affair — everyone knows it!) Then the Gentle Lady will tell you how ungrateful her washwoman was when she gave her a perfectly good, but, of course, a little bit soiled party dress, or a pair of skates for her lame boy, or some such suitable gift at Christmas. She did not act a bit nicely about it!

The Gentle Lady has a very personal and local point of view. She looks at the whole world as related to herself — it all revolves around her, and therefore what she says, or what 'husband' says, is final. She is particularly bitter against the militant suffragette, and excitedly declares they should all be deported.

'I cannot understand them!' she cries.

Therein the Gentle Lady speaks truly. She cannot understand them, for she has nothing to understand them with. It takes nobility of heart to understand nobility of heart. It takes an unselfishness of purpose to understand unselfishness of purpose.

'What do they want?' cries the Gentle Lady. 'Why some of them are rich women — some of them are titled women. Why don't they mind their own business and attend to their own children?'

'But maybe they have no children, or maybe their children, like Mrs. Pankhurst's, are grown up!'

The Gentle Lady will not hear you — will not debate it — she turns to the personal aspect again.

'Well, I am sure *I* have enough to do with my own affairs, and I really have no patience with that sort of thing!'

That settles it!

She does not see, of course, that the new movement among women is a spiritual movement — that women, whose work has been taken away from them, are now beating at new doors, crying to be let in that they may take part in new labors, and thus save womanhood from the enervation which is threatening it. Women were intended to guide and sustain life, to care for the race; not feed on it.

Wherever women have become parasites on the race, it has heralded the decay of that race. History has proven this over and over again. In ancient Greece, in the days of its strength and glory, the women bore their full share of the labor, both manual and mental; not only the women of the poorer classes, but queens and princesses carried water from the well; washed their linen in the stream; doctored and nursed their households; manufactured the clothing for their families; and, in addition to these labors, performed a share of the highest social functions as priestesses and prophetesses.

These were the women who became the mothers of the heroes, thinkers and artists, who laid the foundation of the Greek nation.

In the day of toil and struggle, the race prospered and grew, but when the days of ease and idleness came upon Greece, when the accumulated wealth of subjugated nations, the cheap service of slaves and subject people, made physical labor no longer a necessity; the women grew fat, lazy and unconcerned, and the whole race degenerated, for the race can rise no higher than its women. For a while the men absorbed and reflected the intellectual life, for there still ran in their veins the good red blood of their sturdy grandmothers. But the race was doomed by the indolent, self-indulgent and parasitic females. The women did not all degenerate. Here and there were found women on whom wealth had no power. There was a Sappho, and an Aspasia, who broke out into activity and stood beside their men-folk in intellectual attainment, but the other women did not follow; they were too comfortable, too well fed, too well housed, to be bothered. They had everything — jewels, dresses, slaves. Why worry? They went back to their cushions and rang for tea — or the Grecian equivalent; and so it happened that in the fourth century Greece fell like a rotten tree. Her conqueror was the indomitable Alexander, son of the strong and virile Olympia.

The mighty Roman nation followed in the same path. In the days of her strength, and national health, the women took their full share of the domestic burden, and as well fulfilled important social functions. Then came slave labor, and the Roman woman no longer worked at honorable employment. She did not have to. She painted her face, wore patches on her cheeks, drove in her chariot, and adopted a mincing foolish gait that has come down to us even in this day. Her children were reared by someone else — the nursery governess idea began to take hold. She took no interest in the government of the state, and soon was not fit to take any. Even then, there were writers who saw the danger, and cried out against it, and were not a bit more beloved than the people who proclaim these things now. The writers who told of these things and the dangers to which they were leading unfortunately suggested no remedy. They thought they could drive women back to the water pitcher and the loom, but that was impossible. The clock of time will not turn back. Neither is it by a return to hand-sewing, or a resurrection of quilt-patching that women of the present day will save the race. The old avenues of labor are closed. It is no longer necessary for women to spin and weave, cure meats, and make household remedies, or even fashion the garments for their household. All these things are done in factories. But there are new avenues for women's activities, if we could only clear away the rubbish of prejudice which blocks the entrance. Some women, indeed many women, are busy clearing away the prejudice; many more are eagerly watching from their boudoir windows; many, many more — the 'gentle ladies,' reclining on their couches, fed, housed, clothed by other hands than their own — say: 'What fools these women be!'

There are many women who are already bitten by the poisonous fly of parasitism; there are many women in whose hearts all sense of duty to the race has died, and these belong to many classes. A woman may become a parasite on a very limited amount of money, for the corroding and enervating effect of wealth and comfort sets in just as soon as the individuality becomes clogged, and causes one to rest content from further efforts, on the strength of the labor of someone else. Queen Victoria, in her palace of marble and gold, was able to retain her virility of thought and independence of action as clearly as any pioneer woman who ever battled with conditions, while many a tradesman's wife whose husband gets a raise sufficient for her to keep one maid, immediately goes on the retired list, and lets her brain and muscles atrophy.

The woman movement, which has been scoffed and jeered at and misunderstood most of all by the people whom it is destined to help, is a spiritual revival of the best instincts of womanhood — the instinct to serve and save the race.

Too long have the gentle ladies sat in their boudoirs looking at life in a mirror like the Lady of Shalott, while down below, in the street, the fight rages, and other women, and defenseless children, are getting the worst of it. But the cry is going up to the boudoir ladies to come down and help us, for the battle goes sorely; and many there are who are throwing aside the mirror and coming out where the real things are. The world needs the work and help of the women, and the women must work, if the race will survive.

Chapter 8

Women and the church

Go, labor on, good sister Anne,
   Abundant may thy labors be;
To magnify thy brother man
   Is all the Lord requires of thee!

Go, raise the mortgage, year by year,
   And joyously thy way pursue,
And when you get the title clear,
   We'll move a vote of thanks to you!

Go, labor on, the night draws nigh;
   Go, build us churches — as you can.
The times are hard, but chicken-pie
   Will do the trick. Oh, rustle, Anne!

Go, labor on, good sister Sue,
   To home and church your life devote;
But never, never ask to vote,
   Or we'll be very cross with you!

May no rebellion cloud your mind,
   But joyous let your race be run.
The conference is good and kind
   And knows God's will for every one!

IN DEALING with the relation of women to the church, let me begin properly with a text in Genesis which says: 'God created man in his *own* image ... male and female created he *them.*' That is to say, He created male man and female man. Further on in the story of the creation it says: 'He gave *them* dominion, etc.'

It would seem from this, that men and women got away to a fair start. There was no inequality to begin with. God gave *them* dominion over everything; there were no favors, no special privileges. Whatever inequality has crept in since, has come without God's sanction. It is well to exonerate God from all blame in the matter, for He has been often accused of starting women off with a handicap. The inequality has arisen from men's superior physical strength, which became more pronounced as civilization advanced, and which is only noticeable in the human family. Among all animals, with the possible exception of cattle, the female is quite as large and as well endowed as the male. It is easy for bigger and stronger people to arrogate to themselves a general superiority. Christ came to rebuke the belief that brute strength is the dominant force in life.

It is no wonder that the teachings of Christ make a special appeal to women, for Christ was a true democrat. He made no discrimination between men and women. They were all human beings to Him, with souls to save and lives to live, and He applied to men and women the same rule of conduct.

When the Pharisees brought the woman to Him, accused of a serious crime, insistent that she be stoned at once, Christ turned his attention to them. 'Let him that is without sin among you throw the first stone,' he said. Up to this moment they had been feeling deliciously good, and the contemplation of the woman's sinfulness had given them positive thrills of virtue. But now suddenly each man felt the spotlight on himself, and he winced painfully. Ordinarily they would have bluffed it off, and laughingly declared they were no worse than other men. But the eyes of the Master were on them — kind eyes, patient always, but keen and sharp as a surgeon's knife; and measuring themselves up with the sinless Son of God, their pitiful little pile of respectability fell into irreparable ruin. They forgot all about the woman and her sin as they saw their own miserable sin-eaten, souls, and they slid out noiselessly. When they were gone Christ asked the woman where were her accusers.

'No man hath condemned me, Lord,' she answered truthfully.
'Neither do I condemn you,' He said. 'Go in peace — sin no more!'
I believe that woman did go in peace, and I also believe that she sinned no more, for she had a new vision of manhood, and purity, and love. All at once, life had changed for her.

The Christian Church has departed in some places from Christ's teaching — noticeably in its treatment of women. Christ taught the nobility of loving service freely given; but such a tame uninteresting belief as that did not appeal to the military masculine mind. It declared Christianity was fit only for women and slaves, whose duty and privilege it was lovingly to serve men. The men of Christ's time held His doctrines in contempt. They wanted gratification, praise, glory, applause, action — red blood and raw meat, and this man, this carpenter, nothing but a working man from an obscure village, dared to tell them they should love their neighbor as themselves, that they should bless and curse not.

There was no fun in that! No wonder they began to seek how they could destroy him! Such doctrine was fit for only women and slaves!

It is sometimes stated as a reason for excluding women from the highest courts of the church, that Christ chose men for all of his disciples — that it was to men, and men only, that he gave the command: 'Go ye into the world and preach the gospel to every creature," but that is a very debatable matter. Christ's scribes were all men, and in writing down the sacred story, they would naturally ignore the woman's part of it. It is not more than twenty years ago that in a well-known church paper appeared this sentence, speaking of a series of revival meetings: 'The converted numbered over a hundred souls, exclusive of women and children.' If after nineteen centuries of Christian civilization the scribe ignores women, even in the matter of conversion, we have every reason to believe that Matthew, Mark, Luke or John might easily fail to give women a place 'among those present' or the 'also rans.'

Superior physical force is an insidious thing, and has biased the judgment of even good men. St. Augustine declared woman to be 'a household menace; a daily peril; a necessary evil.' St. Paul, too, added his contribution and advised all men who wished to serve God faithfully to refrain from marriage 'even as I.' 'However,' he said, 'if you feel you must marry, go ahead — only don't say I did not warn you!' Saint Paul is very careful to say that he is giving this advice quite on his own authority, but that has in no way dimmed the faith of those who have quoted it.

Later writers like Sir Almoth Wright declare there are no good women, though there are some who have come under the influence of good men. Many men have felt perfectly qualified to sum up all women in a few crisp sentences, and they do not shrink from declaring in their modest way that they understand women far better than women understand themselves. They love to talk of women in bulk, all women — and quite cheerfully tell us women are illogical, frivolous, jealous, vindictive, forgiving, affectionate, not any too honest, patient, frail, delightful, inconstant, faithful. Let us all take heart of grace for it seems we are the whole thing!

Almost all the books written about women have been written by men. Women have until the last fifty years been the inarticulate sex; but although they have had little to say about themselves they have heard much. It is a very poor preacher or lecturer who has not a lengthy discourse on 'Woman's True Place.' It is a very poor platform performer who cannot take the stand and show women exactly wherein they err. "This way, ladies, for the straight and narrow path!" If women have gone aside from the straight and narrow path it is not because they have not been advised to pursue it. Man long ago decided that woman's sphere was anything he did not wish to do himself, and as he did not particularly care for the straight and narrow way, he felt free to recommend it to women in general. He did not wish to tie himself too close to home either and still he knew somebody should stay on the job, so he decided that home was woman's sphere.

The church has been dominated by men and so religion has been given a masculine interpretation, and I believe the Protestant religion has lost much when it lost the idea of the motherhood of God. There come times when human beings do not crave the calm, even-handed justice of a father nearly so much as the soft-hearted, loving touch of a mother, and to many a man or woman whose home life has not been happy, 'like as a *father* pitieth his children' sounds like a very cheap and cruel sarcasm.

It has been contended by those high in authority in church life, that the admission of women into all the departments of the church will have the tendency to drive men out. Indeed some declare that

the small attendance of men at church services is accounted for by
the 'feminization of the church,' which is, in other words, an
admission of a very ugly fact that even in the sacred precincts of the
church, women are held in mild contempt. Many men will resent this
statement hotly, but a brief glance at some of the conditions which
prevail in our social life will prove that there is a great amount of
truth in it. Look at the fine scorn with which small boys regard girls!
You cannot insult a boy more deeply than to tell him he looks like a
girl — and the bitterest insult one boy can hand out to another is to
call him a 'sissy.' This has been carefully taught to our small boys,
for if they were left to their own observations and deductions they
would hold girls in as high esteem as boys. I remember once seeing a
fond mother buying a coat for her only son, aged seven years. The
salesman had put on a pretty little blue reefer, and the mother was
quite pleased with it, and a sale was apparently in sight. Then the
salesman was guilty of a serious mistake, for as he pulled down the
little coat and patted the shoulders he said: "this is a standard cut,
madam, which is always popular, and we sell a great many of them
for both boys and girls."

Girls!

Reggie's mother stiffened, and with withering scorn declared that
she did not wish Reggie to wear a girl's coat. She would look at
something else. Reggie pulled off the coat, as if it burned him, and
felt he had been perilously near to something very compromising
and indelicate. Thus did young Reggie receive a lesson in sex
contempt at the hands of his mother!

Let us lay the blame where it belongs. If any man holds women in
contempt — and many do — their mothers are to blame for it in the
first place. It began in the nursery but was fostered on the street,
and nourished in the school where sitting with a girl has been handed
out as a punishment, containing the very dregs of humiliation; where
boys are encouraged to play games and have a good time, but where
until a few years ago girls were expected to 'sit around and act
ladylike' in the playtime of the others.

The church has contributed a share, too, in the subjection of
women, in spite of the plain teaching of our Lord, and many a
sermon has been based on the words of Saint Paul about women
remaining silent in the churches, and if any question arose to trouble
her soul, she must ask her husband quietly at home.

But it is at the marriage altar, where women receive the crowning insult. 'Who gives this woman away?' asks the minister. 'I do,' says her father or brother, or some male relative, without a blush. Perfectly satisfactory. One man hands her over to another man, the inference being that the woman has nothing to do with it. In this most vital decision of her whole life, she has had to get a man to do the thinking for her. It goes back to the old days, of course, when a woman was a man's chattel, to do with as he saw fit. The word 'obey' has gone from some of the marriage ceremonies. Bishops even have seen the absurdity of it and taken it out.

Women have held a place all their own in the church. 'I am willing that the sisters should labor,' cried an eminent doctor of the largest Protestant church in Canada, when the question of allowing women to sit in the highest courts of the church was discussed. 'I am willing that the sisters should labor,' he said, 'and that they should labor more abundantly, but we cannot let them rule.' And it was so decreed.

Women have certainly been allowed to labor in the church. There is no doubt of that. There are many things they may do with impunity, nay, even hilarity. They may make strong and useful garments for the poor; they may teach in Sunday-school and attend prayer-meeting; they may finance the new parsonage, and augment the missionary funds by bazaars, birthday socials, autograph quilts and fowl suppers – where the masculine portion of the congregation are given a dollar meal for fifty cents, which they take gladly and generously declare they do not mind the expense for 'it is all for a good cause.' The women may lift mortgages, or build churches, or any other light work, but the real heavy work of the church, such as moving resolutions in the general conference or assemblies, must be done by strong, hardy men!

It is quite noticeable that each of the church dignitaries who have opposed woman's entry into the church courts has prefaced his remarks by elaborate apologies, and never failed to declare his great love for womankind. Each one has bared his manly breast and called the world to witness the fact that he loves his mother and is not ashamed to say so – which declaration is all the more remarkable because no person was asking, or particularly interested in his private affairs. (Query – Why shouldn't he love his mother? Most people do.) After having delivered his soul of these mighty, epoch-making declarations, he has proceeded to explain that letting women into the church would be the thin edge of the wedge, and he is afraid women will 'lose their femininity.'

Women are not discouraged or cast down. Neither have they any intention of going on strike, or withdrawing their support from the church. They will still go on patiently, and earnestly and hopefully. Sex prejudice is a hard thing to break down, and the smaller the man, and the narrower his soul, the more tenaciously will he hold on to his pitiful little belief in his own superiority. The best and ablest men in all the churches are fighting the woman's battles now, and the brotherly companionship, the real chivalry, and fairmindedness of these men, are enough to keep the women's hearts cheered and encouraged. Toward their opponents the women are very tolerant and hopeful. Many of them have changed their beliefs in the last few years. They are changing every day. Those who will not change will die! We always have this assurance, and in this battle for independence, many a woman has found comfort in poor Swinburne's pagan hymn of thanksgiving:

> From too much love of living,
> From fear of death set free,
> We thank thee with brief thanksgiving,
> Whatever gods there be!
> That no life lives forever,
> That dead men rise up never,
> That even the weariest river
> Leads somehow safe to sea!

But when all is over, the battle fought and won, and women are regarded everywhere as human beings and citizens, many women will remember with bitterness that in the day of our struggle, the church stood off, aloof and dignified, and let us fight alone.

One of the arguments advanced by the men who oppose women's entry into the full fellowship of the church is that women would ultimately seek to preach, and the standard of preaching would be lowered. There is a gentle compelling note of modesty about this that is not lost on us — and we frankly admit that we would not like to see the standard of preaching lowered; and we assure the timorous brethren that women are not clamoring to preach; but if a woman should feel that she is divinely called of God to deliver a message, I wonder how the church can be so sure that she isn't. Wouldn't it be perfectly safe to let her have her fling? There was a rule given long ago which might be used yet to solve such a problem: 'And now I say unto you, Refrain from these men, and let them alone, for if this council, or this work, be of men, it will come to naught, but if it be of God you cannot overthrow it, lest haply ye be found even to fight against God.'

That seems to be a pretty fair way of looking at the matter of preaching; but the churches have decreed otherwise, and in order to save trouble they have decided themselves and not left it to God. It must be great to feel that you are on the private wire from heaven and qualified to settle a matter which concerns the spiritual destiny of other people.

Many theories have been propounded as to the decadence of the church, which has become painfully apparent when great moral issues have been at stake. That the church could stamp out the liquor traffic has often been said, and yet although general conferences and assemblies have met year after year, and passed resolutions declaring that 'the sale of liquor could not be licensed without sin,' the liquor traffic goes blithely on its way and gets itself licensed all right, 'with sin,' perhaps, but licensed anyway. Where are all these stalwart sons of the church who love their mothers so ostentatiously and reverence womanhood so deeply?

There is one of Aesop's fables which tells about a man who purchased for himself a beautiful dog, but being a timid man, he was beset with the fear that some day the dog might turn on him and bite him, and to prevent this, he drew all the dog's teeth. One day a wolf attacked the man. He called on his beautiful dog to protect him, but the poor dog had no teeth, and so the wolf ate them both. The church fails to be effective because it has not the use of one wing of its army, and it has no one to blame but itself. The church has deliberately set its face against the emancipation of women, and in that respect it has been a perfect joy to the liquor traffic, who recognize their deadliest foe to be the woman with a ballot in her hand. The liquor traffic rather enjoys temperance sermons, and conventions and resolutions. They furnish an outlet for a great deal of hot talk which hurts nobody.

Of course, various religious bodies in convention assembled have from time to time passed resolutions favoring woman suffrage, and recommending it to the state, but the state has not been greatly impressed. The state might well reply to the church by saying: 'If it is such a desirable thing why do you not try it yourself?'

The antagonism of the church to receiving women preachers has its basis in sex jealousy. I make this statement with deliberation. The smaller the man, the more disposed he is to be jealous. A gentleman of the old school, who believes women should all be housekeepers whether they want to be or not, once went to hear a woman speak; and when asked how he liked it he grudgingly admitted that it was clever enough. He said it seemed to him like a pony walking on its hind legs — it was clever but not natural.

Woman has long been regarded by the churches as helpmate for man, with no life of her own, but a very valuable assistant nevertheless to some male relative. Woman's place they have long been told is to help some man to achieve success and great reward may be hers. Some day when she is faded and old and battered and bent, her son may be pleased to recall her many sacrifices and declare when making his inaugural address: 'All that I am my mother made me!' There are one or two things to be considered in this charming scene. Her son may never arrive at this proud achievement, or even if he does, he may forget his mother and her sacrifices, and again she may not have a son. But these are minor matters.

Children do not need their mother's care always, and the mother who has given up every hope and ambition in the care of her children will find herself left all alone, when her children no longer need her — a woman without a job. But, dear me, how the church has exalted the self-sacrificing mother, who never had a thought apart from her children, and who became a willing slave to her family. Never a word about the injury she is doing to her family in letting them be a slave-owner, never a word of the injury she is doing to herself, never a whisper of the time when the children may be ashamed of their worked-out mother who did not keep up with the times.

The preaching of the church, having been done by men, has given us the strictly masculine viewpoint. The tragedy of the 'willing slave, the living sacrifice,' naturally does not strike a man as it does a woman. A man loves to come home and find his wife or his mother darning his socks. He likes to believe that she does it joyously. It is traditionally correct, and home would not be home without it. No man wants to stay at home too long, but he likes to find his women folks sitting around when he comes home. The stationary female and the wide-ranging male is the world's accepted arrangement, but the belief that a woman must cherish no hope or ambition of her own is both cruel and unjust.

Men have had the control of affairs for a long time, long enough perhaps to test their ability as the arbiters of human destiny. The world, as made by man, is cruelly unjust to women, and cruelly beset with dangers for the innocent young girl. Praying and weeping have been the only weapons that the church has sanctioned for women. The weeping, of course, must be done quietly and in becoming manner. Loud weeping becomes hysteria, and decidedly bad form. Women have prayed and wept for a long time, and yet the liquor traffic and the white slave traffic continue to make their inroads on the human family. The liquor traffic and the white slave traffic are kept up by men for man — women pay the price — the long price in suffering and shame. The pleasure and profit — if there be any — belong to men. Women are the sufferers — and yet the law decrees that women shall not have any voice in regulating these matters.

In California, where women have had the vote for three years, there has been recently enacted a bill dealing with white slavery. It is called the Quick Abatement Act, and provides for an immediate trial to be given, when it is believed that prostitution is being carried on in any house. Our system, under which the trial is set for a date several weeks ahead, furnishes a splendid chance for the witnesses to disappear, and the evidence quite often falls through. This bill also provides a suitable punishment which falls not on the occupants of the house but on the owner of the property, thereby striking at the profit. If prostitution is proven against a house, that house is closed for one year, the owner losing the rent for that time. This puts the responsibility on property owners, and makes people careful as to their tenants. Every owner forthwith becomes a morality officer. This is the greatest and most effective blow ever struck at white slavery, for it strikes directly at the money side of it. It is a fact worth recalling that just before women were permitted to vote in California, this bill was defeated overwhelmingly, but the first time it was submitted after women were enfranchised it passed easily, although there was not one woman in the house of representatives; the men members had a different attitude toward moral matters when they remembered that they had women constituents as well as men.

When Christian women ask to vote, it is in the hope that they may be able with their ballots to protect the weak and innocent, and make the world a safer place for the young feet. As it is now, weakness and innocence are punished more than wickedness.

One of our social workers, going on her rounds, one day met a young Scotch girl, aged nineteen, who belonged to that class of people whom we in our superior way call 'fallen women.' She was a beautiful girl, with curling auburn hair and deep violet eyes. The visitor asked her about herself, but the girl was not disposed to talk. Finally the visitor asked her if she might pray with her. The girl politely refused.

'Lady,' she said wearily, 'what is the use of praying – there is no God. I know that you think there is a God, Lady,' she went on, with a voice of settled sadness. 'I did, too – once – but I know now that there is no God anywhere.'

Then she told her story. When her mother died in Scotland, she came out to Canada to live with her brother who had a position in a bank. She traveled in the care of a Scotch family to her destination. At the station, an elderly gentleman in a clerical coat met her and told her that her brother was ill, but had sent him to meet her. She went with him unsuspectingly. That was six years ago. She was then thirteen years old.

'So you see, Lady,' she said, 'I know there is no God, or He would never have let them do to me what they did. Every night I had prayed to God, and if there were a God anywhere, He would surely have heard my mother's prayer – when she was dying – she asked 'God to protect her poor little motherless girl. It is a sad world, Lady.' The girl's eyes were dry and her voice unbroken. There is a limit even to tears and her eyes were cried dry.

According to the laws of the Dominion of Canada, the man who stole this sweet child from the railway station, would be liable to five years' imprisonment, if the case could be proven against him, which is doubtful, for he could surely get someone to prove that she was over fourteen years of age, or not of previously chaste character, or that he was somewhere else at the time, or that the girl's evidence was contradictory; but if he had stolen any article from any building belonging to or adjacent to a railway station, or any article belonging to a railway company, he would have been liable to a term of fourteen years. This is the law, and the church folds its plump hands over its broadcloth waistcoat and makes no protest! The church has not yet even touched the outer fringe of the white slave evil and yet those high in authority dare to say that women must not be given the right to protect themselves. The demand for votes is a spiritual movement and the bitter cry of that little Scotch girl and of the many like her who have no reason to believe in God, sounds a challenge to every woman who ever names the name of God in prayer. We know there is a God of love and justice, who hears the cry of the smallest child in agony, and will in His own good time bind up every broken heart, and wipe away every tear. But how can we demonstrate God to the world!

Inasmuch as we have sat in our comfortable respectable pews enjoying our own little narrow-gauge religion, unmoved by the call of the larger citizenship, and making no effort to reach out and save those who are in temptation, and making no effort to better the conditions under which other women must live — inasmuch as we have left undone the things we might have done — in God's sight — we are fallen women! And to the church officials, ministers and laymen who have dared to deny to women the means whereby they might have done better for the women of the world, I would like to say that I wonder what they will say to that Scotch mother, who lay down happily on her death-bed believing that God would care for her motherless child left to battle with the world. I wonder how they will explain it to her when they meet her up there! I wonder will they be able to get away with that old fable about their being afraid of women 'losing their femininity.' I wonder!

There is a story recorded in that book, whose popularity never wanes, about a certain poor man who took his journey down from Jerusalem to Jericho, and who fell among thieves who robbed him and left him for dead. A priest and a Levite came along and were full of sympathy, and said: 'Dear me! I wonder what this road is coming to!' But they had meetings to attend and they passed on. A good Samaritan came along, and he was a real good Samaritan, and when he saw the man lying by the road he jumped down from his horse, and picking him up, took him to the inn, and gave directions for his care and comfort, even paid out money for the poor battered stranger. The next day, the Samaritan again passed down the road from Jerusalem to Jericho, and about the same place found another man, beaten and robbed, undoubtedly the work of the same thieves. Again he played the part of the kind friend, but it set him thinking, and when the next day he found two men robbed and beaten, the good Samaritan was properly aroused. He took them to the inn, and again he paid out his money, but that night he called a meeting of all the other good Samaritans 'out his way' and they hunted up their old muskets and set out to clean up the road.

The road from Jerusalem to Jericho is here, and now. Women have played the good Samaritan for a long time, and they have found many a one beaten and robbed on the road of life. They are still doing it, but the conviction is growing on them that it would be much better to go out and clean up the road!

In a certain asylum, the management have a unique test for sanity. When any of the inmates exhibit evidence of returning reason, they submit them to the following tests. Out in the courtyard there are a number of water taps for filling troughs, and to each of the candidates for liberty a small pail is given, and they are told to drain out the troughs, the taps running full force. Some of the poor fellows bail away and bail away, but of course the trough remains full in spite of them. The wise ones turn off the taps.

The women of the churches and many other organizations for many long weary years have been bailing out the troughs of human misery with their little pails; their children's shelters, day nurseries, homes for friendless girls, relief boards, and innumerable public and private charities; but the big taps of intemperance and ignorance and greed are running night and day. It is weary, discouraging, heart-breaking work.

Let us have a chance at the taps!

Chapter 9

The sore thought

The toad beneath the harrow knows
Everywhere the tooth mark goes;
The butterfly upon the road
Preaches contentment to the toad.

WOMEN have had to do a lot of waiting – long, weary waiting. The well-brought-up young lady diligently prepares for marriage; makes doilies, and hem-stitches linen; gets her blue trunk ready and – waits. She must not appear anxious or concerned – not at all; she must just – wait. When a young man comes along and shows her any attention, she may accept it, but if after two or three years of it he suddenly leaves her, and devotes himself to some other girl, she must not feel hurt or grieved but must go back and sit down beside the blue trunk again and – wait! He has merely exercised the man's right of choosing, and when he decides that he does not want her, she has no grounds for complaint. She must consider herself declined, 'not from any lack of merit, but simply because she is unavailable.' If her heart breaks, it must break quietly, and in secret.

She may see a young man to whom she feels attracted, but she must not show it by even so much as the flicker of an eyelash. Hers is the waiting part, and although marriage and homemaking are her highest destiny, or at least so she has been told often enough – she must not raise a hand to help the cause along. No more crushing criticism can be made of a woman, than that she is anxious to get married. It is all right for her to be passively willing, but she must not be anxious.

At dances she must *wait* until someone asks her to dance; *wait* until someone asks her to go to supper. She must not ever make the move – she must not ever try to start something. Her place is to wait!

At last her waiting is rewarded and a young man comes by who declares he would like to marry her, but is not in a position to marry just yet. Then begins another period of waiting. She must not hurry him – that is very indelicate – she must wait. Sometimes, in this long period of waiting, the young man changes his mind, but she must not complain. A man cannot help it if he grows tired. It must have been her fault – she did not make herself sufficiently attractive – that's all! She waits again.

At last perhaps she gets married. But her periods of waiting are not over. Her husband wanders free while she stays at home. We know the picture of the waiting wife listening for footsteps while the clock ticks loudly in the silent house. The world has decreed that the woman and home must stay together, while the man goes about his business or his pleasures – the tied-up woman and the foot-loose man.

Her boys grow up, and when war breaks out, they are called away from her, and again the woman waits. Every telegraph boy who comes up the street may bring the dreaded message; every time the door bell rings her heart stops beating. But she cannot do anything but wait! wait! wait!

Did you ever visit an old folks' home and notice the different spirit shown by the men and women there? The old men are restless and irritable; impatient of their inaction; rebellious against fate. The old women patiently wait, looking out with their dimmed eyes like marooned sailors waiting for a breeze. Poor old patient waiters! you learned the art of waiting in a long hard school, and now you have come to the last lap of the journey.

So they wait — and by and by their waiting will be over, for the kindly tide will rise and bear them safely out on its strong bosom to some place — where they will find not more rest but blessed activity! We know there is another world, because we need it so badly to set this one right!

Women have not always been 'waiters.' There was a day long past, when women chose their mates, when men fought for the hand of the woman they loved, and the women chose. The female bird selects her mate today, goes out and makes her choice, and it is not considered unbirdly either.

Why should not women have the same privilege as men to choose their mate? Marriage means more to a woman than to a man; she brings in a larger contribution than he; often it happens that she gives all — he gives nothing. The care and upbringing of the children depend upon her faithfulness, not on his. Why should she not have the privilege of choosing?

Too long has the whole process of love-making and marriage been wrapped in mystery. 'Part of it has been considered too holy to be spoken of and part of it too unholy,' says Charlotte Perkins Gilman. Innocence has been esteemed a young girl's greatest charm, but what good has her innocence done her? No good at all! It is not calculated to do her good — her good is not the prime consideration. It makes her more charming in the eyes of men; but it may bring her great unhappiness. Lady Evelyn's trusting heart has usually been broken. When the story begins about the farmer's pretty daughter with limpid blue eyes, sweet as bluebells washed in dew, all innocent of the world ways, the experienced reader knows at once what is coming. Innocence is hard on the woman, however charming it may be to men. The women who go a step beyond innocence and are so trusting as to be described as simple-minded, no matter how gentle, patient, and sweet they are, are absolutely unsafe in this world of man's chivalry and protection. If you want to know what fate overtakes them, ask the matron of the Refuge for Unfortunate Women, ask any person who has worked among this class of women, and they will tell you how much good innocence and the trusting heart does any woman. This is a sore thought!

It would be perfectly delightful if our daughters might remain innocent. They should have that privilege. Innocence belongs to childhood and girlhood, but under present conditions, it is as dangerous and foolish as level and unguarded railway crossings, or open and unguarded trap doors. It is no pleasant task to have to tell a joyous, sunny-hearted girl of fourteen or fifteen about the evils that are in the world, but if you love her, you will do it! I would like to see this work done by trained motherly and tactful women, in the department of social welfare, paid by the school board. I know the mothers should do it, but many mothers are ignorant, foolish, lax, and certainly untrained. The mother's kindly counsel is the best, I know, but you cannot always rely upon its being there. This is coming, too, for public sentiment is being awakened to the evils of innocence.

I remember, twenty years ago, when Dr. Amelia Yeomans, of sainted memory, published at her own expense, a little leaflet called 'Warning to Girls' and circulated it among girls who were working in public places, what a storm of abuse arose. I have a copy of the little tract, and it could be safely read in any mixed gathering today. Ministers raged against it in the pulpit. I remember one brother who was very emphatic in his denunciations who afterwards was put out of the church for indecent conduct. Of course he wanted girls to remain innocent — it suited his purpose.

If any person doubts that the society of the present day has been made by men, and for men's advantage, let them look for a minute at the laws which govern society. Society allows a man all privilege, all license, all liberty, where women are concerned. He may lie to women, deceive them — 'all's fair in love and war' — he may break many a heart, and blast many a fair name; that merely throws a glamour around him. 'He's a devil with women,' they say, and it is no disadvantage in the business or political world – where man dominates. But if a man is dishonest in business or neglects to pay his gambling bills, he is down and out. These are crimes against men – and therefore serious. This is also a sore thought!

Then when men speak of these things, they throw the blame on women themselves, showing thereby that the Garden of Eden story of Adam and Eve and the apple, whether it be historically true or not, is true to life. Quite Adam-like, they throw the blame on women, and say: 'Women like the man with a past. Women like to be lied to. Women do not expect any man to be absolutely faithful to them, if he is pleasant. The man who has the reputation of having been wild has a better chance with women than the less attractive but absolutely moral man.' What a glorious thing it will be when men cease to speak for us, and cease to tell us what we think, and let us speak for ourselves!

Since women's sphere of manual labor has so narrowed by economic conditions and has not widened correspondingly in other directions, many women have become parasites on the earnings of their male relatives. Marriage has become a straight 'clothes and board' proposition to the detriment of marriage and the race. Her economic dependence has so influenced the attitude of some women toward men, that it is the old man with the money who can support her in idleness who appeals to her far more than the handsome, clean-limbed young man who is poor, and with whom she would have to work. The softening, paralyzing effects of ease and comfort are showing themselves on our women. You cannot expect the woman who has had her meals always bought for her, and her clothes always paid for by some man, to retain a sense of independence. 'What did I marry you for?' cried a woman indignantly, when her husband grumbled about the size of her millinery bill. No wonder men have come to regard marriage as an expensive adventure.

The time will come, we hope, when women will be economically free, and mentally and spiritually independent enough to refuse to have their food paid for by men; when women will receive equal pay for equal work, and have all avenues of activity open to them; and will be free to choose their own mates, without shame, or indelicacy; when men will not be afraid of marriage because of the financial burden, but free men and free women will marry for love, and

together work for the sustenance of their families. It is not too ideal
a thought. It is coming, and the new movement among women who
are crying out for a larger humanity, is going to bring it about.

But there are many good men who view this with alarm. They are
afraid that if women were economically independent they would
never marry. But they would. Deeply rooted in almost every
woman's heart is the love of home and children; but independence is
sweet and when marriage means the loss of independence, there are
women brave enough and strong enough to turn away from it. 'I will
not marry for a living,' many a brave woman has said.

The world has taunted women into marrying. So odious has the
term 'old maid' been in the past that many a woman has married
rather than have to bear it. That the term 'old maid' has lost its
odium is due to the fact that unmarried women have made a place
for themselves in the world of business. They have become real
people apart from their sex. The 'old maid' of the past was a sad,
anemic creature, without any means of support except the bounty
of some relative. She had not married, so she had failed utterly, and
the world did not fail to rub it in. The unmarried woman of today is
the head saleslady in some big house, drawing as big a salary as most
men, and the world kowtows to her. The world is beginning to see
that a woman may achieve success in other departments of life as
well as marriage.

It speaks well for women that, even before this era, when 'old
maids' were open to all kinds of insult, there were women brave
enough to refuse to barter their souls for the animal comforts of
food and shelter. Speaking about 'old maids,' by which term we
mean now a prim, fussy person, it is well to remember that there are
male 'old maids' as well as female who remain so all through life;
also that many 'old maids' marry, and are still old maids.

When women are free to marry or not as they will, and the
financial burden of making a home is equally shared by husband and
wife, the world will enter upon an era of happiness undreamed of
now. As it is now, the whole matter of marrying and homemaking is
left to chance. Every department of life, every profession in which
men and women engage, has certain qualifications which must be
complied with, except the profession of homemaking. A young man
and a young woman say: 'I believe we'll get married' and forthwith
they do. The state sanctions it, and the church blesses it. They may

be consumptive, epileptic, shiftless, immoral, or with a tendency to insanity. No matter. They may go on and reproduce their kind. They are perfectly free to bring children into the world, who are a burden and a menace to society. Society has to bear it — that is all! 'Be fruitful and multiply!' declares the church, as it deplores the evils of race suicide. Many male moralists have cried out for large families. 'Let us have better and healthier babies if we can,' cried out one of England's bishops, not long ago, 'but let us have more babies!'

Heroic and noble sentiment and so perfectly safe! It reminds one of the dentist's advertisement: 'Teeth extracted without pain' — and his subsequent explanation: 'It does not hurt *me* a bit!'

Martin Luther is said to have stood by the deathbed of a woman, who had given birth to sixteen children in seventeen years, and piously exclaimed: 'She could not have died better!'

'By all means let us have more babies,' says the Bishop. Even if they are anemic and rickety, ill-nourished and deformed, and even if the mothers, already overburdened and underfed, die in giving them birth? To the average thinking woman, this wail for large families, coming as it always does from men, is rather nauseating.

When the cry has been so persistently raised for more children, the women naturally wonder why more care is not exerted for the protection of the children who are already here. The reason is often given for not allowing women to have the free grants of land in Canada on the same conditions as men, that it would make them too independent of marriage, and, as one commissioner of emigration phrased it: 'It is not independent women we want; it is population.'

Granting that population is very desirable, would it not be well to save what we have? Six or seven thousand of our population in Canada drop out of the race every year as a direct result of the liquor traffic, and a higher percentage than this perish from the same cause in some other countries. Would it not be well to save them? Thousands of babies die every year from preventable causes. Free milk depositories and district nurses and free dispensaries would save many of them. In the Far West, on the border of civilization, where women are beyond the reach of nurses and doctors, many mothers and babies die every year. How would it be to try to save them? Delegations of public-spirited women have waited upon august bodies of men, and pleaded the cause of these brave women who are paying the toll of colonization, and have asked that Government nurses be sent to them in their hour of need. But up to date not one dollar of Government money has been spent on them notwithstanding the fact that when a duke or a prince comes to visit our country, we can pour out money like water!

It does not seem to the thoughtful observer that we need more children nearly so much as we need better children, and a higher value set upon all human life. In this day of war, when men are counted of less value than cattle, it is a doubtful favor to the child to bring it into life under any circumstances, but to bring children into the world, suffering from the handicaps caused by the ignorance, poverty, or criminality of the parents, is an appalling crime against the innocent and helpless, and yet one about which practically nothing is said. Marriage, homemaking, and the rearing of children are left entirely to chance, and so it is no wonder that humanity produces so many specimens who, if they were silk stockings or boots, would be marked 'Seconds.' The Bishop's cry has found many an echo: 'Let us have more.'

Women in several of the states have instituted campaigns for 'Better Babies,' and by offering prizes and disseminating information, they have given a better chance to many a little traveler on life's highway. But all who have endeavored in any way to secure legislation or government grants for the protection of children, have found that legislators are more willing to pass laws for the protection of cattle than for the protection of children, for cattle have a real value and children have only a sentimental value.

If children die — what of it? 'The Lord gave and the Lord hath taken away.' Let us have more. This is the sore thought with women. It is not that the bringing of children into the world is attended with pain and worry and weariness — it is not that: it is that they are held of such small value in the eyes of this man-made world. This is the sorest thought of all!

Even as I write these words, I hear the bugle calling, and down the street our brave boys in khaki are marching. Today I passed on the street a mother and her only son, who is now a soldier and going away with the next contingent. The lad was trying to cheer her as they walked along. She held him by the hand — he was just a little boy to her.

'It was not for this that I raised him,' she said to me bitterly. 'It was not for this! The whole thing is wrong, and it is just as hard on the German women as on us!'

Even in her sorrow she had the universal outlook – the very thing that so many philosophers declare that women have not got!

I could not help but think that if there had been women in the German Reichstag, women with authority behind them, when the Kaiser began to lay his plans for the war, the results might have been very different. I do not believe women with boys of their own would ever sit down and wilfully plan slaughter, and if there had been women there when the Kaiser and his brutal war-lords discussed the way in which they would plunge all Europe into bloodshed, I believe one of those deep-bosomed, motherly, blue-eyed German women would have stood upon her feet and said: 'William – forget it!' But the German women were not there – they were at home, raising children! So the preparations for war went on unchecked, and the resolutions passed without a dissenting voice. In German rule, we have a glorious example of male statecraft, uncontaminated by any feminine foolishness.

No doubt, it is because all our statecraft has been one-sided, that we find that human welfare has lagged far behind material welfare. We have made wonderful strides in convenience and comfort, but have not yet solved the problems of poverty, crime or insanity. Perhaps they, too, will yield to treatment when they are better understood, and men and women are both on the job. As it is now, criminals have only man's treatment, which is the hurry-up method – 'hang him, and be done with him,' or 'chuck him into jail, and be quick about it, and let me forget him.' Mothers would have more patience, more understanding, for they have been dealing with bad little boys all their lives.

The little family jars which arise in every home, are settled nine out of ten times by the mother, unless she is the sort of spineless, anemic woman, who lies down on the job, and says, 'I'll tell your father,' which acts as a threat, and sometimes is effective, though it solves no difficulty.

To hang the man who commits a crime is a cheap way to get out of a difficulty; a real masculine way. It is so much quicker and easier than trying to reform him, and what is one man less after all? Human life is cheap – to men – and of course there is always the Bishop crying: 'Let us have more.'

The conditions which prevail at the present time are atrocious and help to make criminals. The worst crimes have not even a name yet, much less a punishment. What about the crime of working little children and cheating them out of an education and a happy childhood? There is no name for it! What about misrepresenting land values and selling lots to people who have never seen them and who simply rely upon the owner's word; taking the hard-earned money from guileless people and giving them swamp land, miles out of the city limits, in return! They tell a story about a real-estate man who sold Edmonton lots to some people in the East, assuring them that the lots were 'close in,' but when the owner of the lots went to register them, he found they could not be registered in Alberta — they belonged in British Columbia, the next province!

This sort of thing is considered good business, if you can 'get away with it.' According to our masculine code of morals — it's rather clever' — they say. 'You cannot help but admire his nerve!' But not long since a hungry man stole a banana from a fruit stand and was sent to jail for it, for the dignity of the law has to be upheld, and the small thief is the easiest one to deal with and make an example of. Similarly Chinamen are always severely dealt with. Give it to him! He has no friends!

What about the crime of holding up the market, so that the price of bread goes up, causing poor men's children to go hungry? There is no name for it!

What about allowing speculators to hold great tracts of land uncultivated, waiting for higher prices, while unemployed men walk the streets, hungry and discouraged, cursing the day they were born: big strong fellows many of them, willing to work, craving work, but with work denied them. Yesterday one of them jumped from the High Level Bridge into the icy waters of the Saskatchewan, leaving a note behind him saying simply he was tired of it all, and could stand no more — he 'would take a chance on another world.' The idle land is calling to the idle man, and the world is calling for food; and yet these great tracts of wheat lands lie just outside our cities, untouched by plow or harrow, and hungry men walk our streets. The crime which the state commits in allowing such a condition to prevail is as yet un-named.

Women have carried many a sore thought in their hearts, feeling that they have been harshly dealt with by their men folk, and have laid the blame on the individual man, when in reality the individual has not been to blame. The whole race is suffering from masculinity; and men and women are alike to blame for tolerating it.

The baby girl in her cradle gets the first cold blast of it. 'A girl?' says the kind neighbor, 'Oh, too bad – I am sure it was quite a disappointment!'

Then there is the old-country reverence for men, of which many a mother has been guilty, which exalts the boys of the family far above the girls, and brings home to the latter, in many, many ways, the grave mistake of having been born a woman. Many little girls have carried the sore thought in their hearts from their earliest recollection.

They find out, later, that women's work is taken for granted. A farmer will allow his daughter to work many weary unpaid years, and when she gets married he will give her 'a feather bed and a cow,' and feel that her claim upon him has been handsomely met. The gift of a feather bed is rather interesting, too, when you consider that it is the daughter who has raised the geese, plucked them, and made the bed-tick. But 'father' gives it to her just the same. The son, for a corresponding term of service, gets a farm.

There was a rich farmer once, who died possessed of three very fine farms of three hundred and twenty acres each. He left a farm to each of his three sons. To his daughter Martha, a woman of forty years of age, the eldest of the family, who had always stayed at home, and worked for the whole family – he left a cow and one hundred dollars. The wording of the will ran: 'To my dear daughter, Martha, I leave the sum of one hundred dollars, and one cow named 'Bella.' '

How would you like to be left at forty years of age, with no training and very little education, facing the world with one hundred dollars and one cow, even if she were named 'Bella'?

To the poor old mother, sixty-five years of age, who had worked far harder than her husband, who had made butter, and baked bread, and sewed carpet rags, and was now bent and broken, and with impaired sight, he left: 'her keep' with one of the boys!

How would you like to be left with 'your keep' even with one of your own children? Keep! It is exactly what the humane master leaves to an old horse. When the old lady heard the will read which so generously provided for her 'keep,' she slipped away without a word. People thought it was her great grief at losing such a kind husband which made her pine and droop. But it wasn't. It was the loss of her independence. Her son and his family thought it strange

that 'Grandma' did not care to go to church any more. Of course her
son never thought of giving her collection or money to give to the
funds of the church, and Grandma did not ask. She sat in her corner,
and knit stockings for her son's children; another pitiful little broken
bit of human wreckage cast up by the waves of the world. In two
months Grandma had gone to the house of many mansions, where
she was no longer beholden to anyone for 'keep' — for God is more
merciful than man!

The man who made his will this way was not a bad man, but he
was the victim of wrong thinking; he did not realize that his wife had
any independence of soul; he thought that all 'mother' cared about
was a chance to serve; she had been a quiet, unassertive woman, who
worked along patiently, and made no complaint. What could she
need of money? The 'boys' would never see her want.

A man who heard this story said in comment: 'Well, I don't see
what the old lady felt so badly about, for what does a woman of
sixty-five need of money anyway?'

He was not a cruel man, either, and so his remark is illuminative,
for it shows a certain attitude of mind, and it shows women where
they have made their mistake. They have been too patient and
unassertive — they have not set a high enough value on themselves,
and it is pathetically true that the world values you at the value you
place on yourself. And so the poor old lady, who worked all her life
for her family, looking for no recompense, nor recognition, was
taken at the value she set upon herself, which was nothing at all.

That does not relieve the state of its responsibility in letting such
a thing happen. It is a hard matter, I know, to protect people from
themselves; and there can be no law made to prevent women from
making slaves of themselves to their husbands and families. That
would be interfering with the sanctity of the home! But the law can
step in, as it has in some provinces, and prevent a man from leaving
his wife with only 'her keep.' The law is a reflection of public
sentiment, and when people begin to realize that women are human
and have human needs and ambitions and desires, the law will
protect a woman's interest. Too long we have had this condition of
affairs: 'Ma' has been willing to work without any recompense, and
'Pa and the boys' have been willing to let her.

Of course, I know, sentimental people will cry out, that very few
men would leave their wives in poverty — I know that; men are

infinitely better than the law, but we must remember that laws are not made to govern the conduct of good men. Good men will do what is right, if there were never a law; but, unfortunately, there are some men who are not good, and many more who are thoughtless and unintentionally cruel. The law is a schoolmaster to such.

There are some places, where a law can protect the weak, but there are many situations which require more than a law. Take the case of a man who habitually abuses and frightens his family, and makes their lives a periodic hell of fear. The law cannot touch him unless he actually kills some of them, and it seems a great pity that there cannot be some corrective measure. In the states of Kansas and Washington (where women vote) the people have enacted what is known as the 'Lazy Husband's Act,' which provides for such cases as this. If a man is abusive or disagreeable, or fails to provide for his family, he is taken away for a time, and put to work in a state institution, and his money is sent home to his family. He is treated kindly, and good influences thrown around him. When he shows signs of repentance – he is allowed to go home. Home, very often, looks better to him, and he behaves himself quite decently.

Women outlined this legislation and it is in the states where women vote that it is in operation. There will be more such legislation, too, when women are given a chance to speak out!

A New Zealander once wrote home to a friend in England advising him to fight hard against woman suffrage. 'Don't ever let the wimmin vote, Bill,' he wrote. 'They are good servants, but bad masters. Over there you can knock your wife about for five shillings, but here we does jail for it!'

The man who 'knocks his wife about' or feels that he might some day want to knock her about, is opposed to further liberties for women, of course.

But that is the class of man from whom we never expected anything. He has his prototype, too, in every walk of life. Don't make the mistake of thinking that only ignorant members of the great unwashed masses talk and feel this way. Silk-hatted 'noblemen' have answered women's appeals for common justice by hiring the Whitechapel toughs to 'bash their heads,' and this is another sore thought that women will carry with them for many a day after the suffrage has been granted. I wish we could forget the way our English sisters have been treated in that sweet land of liberty!

The problems of discovery have been solved; the problems of colonization are being solved, and when the war is over the problem of world government will be solved; and then the problem will be just the problem of living together. That problem cannot be solved without the help of women. The world has suffered long from too much masculinity and not enough humanity, but when the war is over, and the beautiful things have been destroyed, and the lands laid desolate, and all the blood has been shed, the poor old bruised and broken heart of the world will cry out for its mother and nurse, who will dry her own eyes, and bind up its wounds and nurse it back to life once more. Perhaps the old earth will be a bit kinder than it has ever been to women, who knows? Men have been known to grow very fond of their nurse, and bleeding has been known to cure mental disorders!

Chapter 10

The land of the fair deal

Lord, take us up to the heights, and show us the glory,
Show us a vision of Empire! Tell us its story!
Tell it out plain, for our eyes and our ears have grown holden;
We have forgotten that anything other than money is golden.
Grubbing away in the valley, somehow has darkened our eyes;
Watching the ground and the crops — we've forgotten the skies.
But Lord, if Thou wilt Thou canst take us today
    To the Mount of Decision
And show us the land that we live in
    With glorified Vision!

EVERY nation has its characteristic quality of mind; we recognize Scotch thrift, English persistency and Irish quickwittedness wherever we see it; we know something, too, of the emotional, vivacious nature of the French, and the resourcefulness of the American; but what about the Canadian — what will be our distinguishing feature in the years to come? The cartoons are kind to us — thus far — and in representing Canada, draw a sturdy young fellow, strong and well set, full of muscle and vim, and we like to think that the representation is a good one, for we are a young nation, coming into our vigor, and with our future in our own hands. We have an area of one-third of the whole British Empire, and one-fifth of that of Asia. Canada is as large as thirty United Kingdoms and eighteen Germanys. Canada is almost as large as Europe. It is bounded by three oceans and has thirteen thousand miles of coast line, that is, half the circumference of the earth.

Canada's land area, exclusive of forest and swamp lands, is 1,401,000,000 acres; 440,000,000 acres of this is fit for cultivation, but only 36,000,000 acres, or 2.6 per cent of the whole, is cultivated, so it would seem that there are still a few acres left for anyone who may happen to want it. We need not be afraid of crowding. We have a great big blank book here with leather binding and gold edges, and now our care should be that we write in it worthily. We have no precedents to guide us, and that is a glorious thing, for precedents, like other guides, are disposed to grow tyrannical, and refuse to let us do anything on our own initiative. Life grows wearisome in the countries where precedents and conventionalities rule, and nothing can happen unless it has happened before. Here we do not worry about precedents — we make our own!

Main Street, in Winnipeg, now one of the finest business streets in the world, followed the trail made by the Red River carts, and, no doubt, if the driver of the first cart knew that in his footsteps would follow electric cars and asphalt paving, he would have driven straighter. But he did not know, and we do not blame him for that. But we know, for in our short day we have seen the prairies blossom into cities, and we know that on the paths which we are marking out many feet will follow, and the responsibility is laid on us to lay them broad and straight and safe so that many feet may be saved from falling.

We are too young a nation yet to have any distinguishing characteristic and, of course, it would not be exactly modest for us to attribute virtues to ourselves, but there can be harm in saying what we would like our character to be. Among the people of the world in the years to come, we will ask no greater heritage for our country than to be known as the land of the Fair Deal, where every race, color and creed will be given exactly the same chance; where no person can 'exert influence' to bring about his personal ends; where no man or woman's past can ever rise up to defeat them; where no crime goes unpunished; where every debt is paid; where no prejudice is allowed to masquerade as a reason; where honest toil will insure an honest living; where the man who works receives the reward of his labor.

It would seem reasonable, too, that such a condition might be brought about in a new country, and in a country as big as ours, where there is room for everyone and to spare. Look out upon our rolling prairies, carpeted with wild flowers, and clotted over with poplar groves, where wild birds sing and chatter, and it does not seem too ideal or visionary that these broad sunlit spaces may be the homes of countless thousands of happy and contented people. The great wide uncultivated prairie seems to open its welcoming arms to the land-hungry, homeless dwellers of the cities, saying: 'Come and try me. Forget the past, if it makes you sad. Come to me, for I am the Land of the Second Chance. I am the Land of Beginning Again. I will not ask who your ancestors were. I want you — nothing matters now but just you and me, and we will make good together.' This is the invitation of the prairie to the discouraged and weary ones of the older lands, whose dreams have failed, whose plans have gone wrong, and who are ready to fall out of the race. The blue skies and green slopes beckon to them to come out and begin again. The prairie, with its peace and silence, calls to the troubled nations of Middle Europe, whose people are caught in the cruel tangle of war. When it is all over and the smoke has cleared away, and they who are left look around at the blackened ruins and desolated farms and the shallow graves of their beloved dead, they will come away from the scenes of such bitter memories. Then it is that this far country will make its appeal to them, and they will come to us in large numbers, come with their sad hearts and their sad traditions. What will we have for them? We have the fertility of soil; we have the natural resources;

we have coal; we have gas; we have wheat land and pasture land and fruit land. Nature has done her share with a prodigality that shames our little human narrowness. Now if we had men to match our mountains, if we had men to match our plains, if our thoughts were as clear as our sunlight, we would be able to stand up high enough to see over the rim of things. In the light of what has happened, our little grabbing ways, our insane desires to grow rich and stop work, have some way lost their glamour. Belgium has set a pace for us, has shown us a glimpse of heroic sacrifice which makes us feel very humble and very small, and we have suddenly stumbled on the great truth that it is not all of life to live, that is, draw your breath or even draw your salary; that to get money and dress your family up like Christmas trees, and own three cars, may not be adding a very heavy contribution to human welfare; that houses and lands and stocks and shares may be very poor things to tie up to after all.

An Englishman who visited Western Canada a few years ago, when everybody had money, wrote letters to one of the London papers about us. Commenting on our worldliness, he said: 'The people of Western Canada have only one idea of hell, and that is buying the wrong lots!'

But already there has come a change in the complexion of our mind. The last eight months have taught us many things. We, too, have had our share in the sacrifice, as the casualty lists in every paper show. We have seen our brave lads go out from us in health and hope, amid music and cheers, and already we know that some of them will not come back. 'Killed in action,' 'died of wounds,' 'missing,' say the brief despatches, which tell us that we have made our investment of blood. The investment thus made has paid a dividend already, in an altered thought, a chastened spirit, a recast of our table of values. 'Without the shedding of blood, there is no remission of sin' always seemed a harsh and terrible utterance, but we know now its truth; and already we know the part of our sin of worldliness has been remitted, for we have turned away from it. We acknowledge in sorrow that we have followed strange gods, and worshiped at the worldly altar of wealth and cleverness, and believed that these things were success in life. Now we have had before our eyes the spectacle of clever men using their cleverness to kill, maim and destroy innocent women and children; we have seen the wealth of one nation poured out like water to bring poverty and starvation

to another nation, and so, through our tears, we have learned the
lesson that it is not wealth or cleverness or skill or power which
makes a nation or an individual great. It is goodness, gentleness,
kindliness, the sense of brotherhood, which alone maketh rich and
addeth no sorrow. When we are face to face with the elemental
things of life, death and sorrow and loss, the air grows very still and
clear, and we see things in bold outlines.

The Kaiser has done a few things for us. He has made us hate all
forms of tyranny and oppression and autocracy; he has made us hate
all forms of hypocrisy and deceit. There have been some forms of
kaiserism dwelling among us for many years, so veneered with
respectability and custom that some were deceived by them; but the
lid is off now – the veneer has cracked – the veil is torn, and we
see things as they are.

When we find ourselves wondering at the German people for
having tolerated the military system for so long, paying taxes for its
maintenance and giving their sons to it, we suddenly remember that
we have paid taxes and given our children, too, to keep up the liquor
traffic, which has less reasons for its existence than the military
system of Germany. Any nation which sets out to give a fair deal to
everyone must divorce itself from the liquor traffic, which deals its
hardest blows on the non-combatants. Right here let us again thank
the Germans for bringing this so clearly to our notice. We despise the
army of the Kaiser for dropping bombs on defenseless people, and
shooting down women and children – we say it violates all laws of
civilized warfare. The liquor traffic has waged war on women and
children all down the centuries. Three thousand women were killed
in the United States in one year by their own husbands who were
under the influence of liquor. Non-combatants! Its attacks on the
non-combatants are not so spectacular in their methods as the tactics
pursued by the Kaiser's men, who line up the defenseless ones in the
public square and turn machine-guns on them. The methods of the
liquor traffic are not so direct or merciful. We shudder with horror
as we read of the terrible outrages committed by the brutal German
soldiers. We rage in our helpless fury that such things should
be – and yet we have known and read of just such happenings in our
own country. The newspapers, in telling of such happenings, usually
have one short illuminative sentence which explains all: 'The man
had been drinking.' The liquor traffic has outraged and insulted

womanhood right here in our own country in much the same manner as is alleged of the German soldiers in France and Belgium! Another thing we have to thank the Kaiser for is that we have something now whereby we can express what women owe to the liquor traffic. We know now that women owe to the liquor traffic the same sort of a debt that Belgium owes to Germany. Women have never chosen the liquor business, have never been consulted about it in any way, any more than Belgium was consulted. It has been wished on them. They have had nothing to do with it, but to put up with it, endure it, suffer its degradation, bear its losses, pay its abominable price in tears and heartbreak. Apart from that they have had nothing to do with it. If there is any pleasure in it — that has belonged to men; if there has been any gain in it, men have had that, too.

And yet there are people who tell us women must not invade the realm of politics, where matters relating to the liquor traffic are dealt with. Women have not been the invaders. The liquor traffic has invaded woman's place in life. The shells have been dropped on unfortified homes. There is no fair dealing in that.

A woman stooped over her stove in her own kitchen one winter evening, making food for her eight-months-old baby, whom she held in her arms. Her husband and her brother-in-law, with a bottle of whiskey, carried on a lively dispute in another part of the kitchen. She did not enter into the dispute, but went on with her work. Surely this woman was protected; here was the sacred precincts of home, her husband, sworn to protect her, her child in her arms — a beautiful domesticated Madonna scene. But when the revolver was fired accidentally it blew off the whole top of her protected head; and the mother and babe fell to the floor! Who was the invader? and, tell me, would you call that a fair deal?

The people who oppose democratic principles tell us that there is no such thing as equality — that, if you made every person exactly equal today, there would be inequality tomorrow. We know there is no such thing as equality of achievement, but what we plead for is equality of chance, equality of opportunity.

We know that absolute equality of opportunity is hardly possible, but we can make it more nearly possible by the removal of all movable handicaps from the human race. The liquor traffic, with its resultant poverty, hits the child in the cradle, whose innocence and helplessness makes its appeal all the stronger. The liquor traffic is a tangible, definite thing that we can locate without difficulty. Many of the causes of poverty and sin are illusive, indefinite qualities such as bad management, carelessness, laziness, extravagance, ignorance and bad judgment, which are exceedingly hard to remedy, but the liquor traffic is one of the things we can speak of definitely, and in removing it we are taking a step in the direction of giving everybody a fair start.

When the Boer War was on, the British War Office had to lower the standard for the army because not enough men could be found to measure up to the previous standard, and an investigation was made into the causes which had led to the physical deterioration of the race. Ten families whose parents were both drinkers were compared with ten families whose parents were both abstainers, and it was found that the drinking parents had out of their fifty-seven children only ten that were normal, while the non-drinking parents, out of their sixty-one children, had fifty-four normal children and only seven that were abnormal in any way. They chose families in as nearly as possible the same condition of life and the same scale of intelligence. It would seem from this that no country which legalizes the liquor traffic is giving a fair deal to its children!

Humanity is disposed to sit weakly down before anything that has been with us for a long time, and say it is impossible to do away with it. 'We have always had liquor drinking,' say some, 'and we always will. It is deeply rooted in our civilization and in our social customs, and can never be outlawed entirely.' Social customs may change. They have changed. They will change when enough people want them to change. There is nothing sacred about a social custom, anyway, that it should be preserved when we have decided it is of no use to us. Social customs make an interesting psychological study, even among the lower animals, who show an almost human respect for the customs of their kind.

Have you ever seen lizards walk into a campfire? Up from the lake they will come, attracted by the gleam of the fire. It looks so warm and inviting, and, of course, there is a social custom among lizards to walk right in, and so they do. The first one goes boldly in, gives a start of surprise, and then shrivels, but the next one is a real good sport, and won't desert a friend, so he walks in and shrivels, and the next one is no piker, so walks in, too. Who would be a stiff?

They stop coming when there are no more lizards in the lake or the fire is full. There does not seem to be much reason for their action, but, of course, it is a social custom. You may have been disposed to despise the humble lizard with his open countenance and foolish smile, but you see there is something quite human and heroic about him, too, in his respect for a social custom.

Moths have a social custom, too, which impels them to fly into the flame of the candle, and bees will drown themselves in boiling syrup. No matter how many of their friends and cousins they see lying dead in the syrup, they will march boldly in, for they each feel that they are strong enough to get out when they want to. Bees all believe that they 'can drink or leave it alone.'

But moralists tell us that prohibition of any evil is not the right method to pursue; far better to leave the evil and train mankind to shun it. If the evil be removed entirely mankind will be forced to abstain and therefore will not grow in strength. In other words, the life of virtue will be made too easy. We would gently remind the moralists who reason in this way that there will still be a few hundred ways left, whereby a man may make shipwreck of his life. They must not worry about that — there will still be plenty of opportunities to go wrong!

The object of all laws should be to make the path of virtue as easy as possible, to build fences in front of all precipices, to cover the wells and put the poison out of reach. The theory of teaching children to leave the poison alone sounds well, but most of us feel we haven't any children to experiment on, and so we will lock the medicine-chest and carry the key.

A great deal is said about personal liberty in connection with this matter of the prohibition of the liquor traffic, though the old cry that every man has a perfect right to do as he likes is not so popular as it once was, for we have before us a perfect example of a man who is exercising personal liberty to the full; we have one man who is a living exponent of the right to do exactly as he likes, no matter who is hurt by it. The perfect example of a man who believes in personal liberty for himself is a man by the name of William Hohenzollern.

If there were only one man on the earth, he might have personal liberty to do just as he liked, but the advent of the second man would end it. Life is full of prohibitions to which we must submit for the good of others. Our streets are full of prohibitory signs, every one of which infringes on our so-called personal liberty: 'Keep off the grass,' 'Go slow,' 'No smoking,' 'Do not feed the animals,' 'Post no bills,' 'Kindly refrain from conversation.'

Those who profess to understand the human heart in all its workings, notably beer-drinking bishops and brewers, declare that a prohibitory measure rouses opposition in mankind. When the law says, 'Thou shalt not,' the individual replies, 'I certainly shall!' This is rather an unkind cut at the ten commandments, which were given by divine authority, and which make a lavish use of 'Thou shalt not!' These brave souls, who feel such a desire to break every prohibition, must have a hard time keeping out of jail. No doubt it is with difficulty that they restrain themselves from climbing over the railway gates which are closed when the train comes in and which block the street for a few minutes several times a day.

The Archbishop of York, speaking at the York Convention recently, declared against prohibition on the ground that when the prohibition was removed there might be 'real and regrettable intemperance' – the inference being that any little drinking that is going on now is of an imaginary and trifling nature – and yet the Chancellor of the Exchequer declares that the liquor traffic is a worse enemy than the Germans, and Earl Kitchener has added his testimony to the same sentiment.

The Dean of Canterbury declared that he did not believe in prohibition, for he once tried total abstinence and he found it impaired his health. Of course the Dean's health must be kept up whether the warships are built or not. England may be suffering from loss of men, money and efficiency, but why worry? The Dean's health is excellent! When we pray for the erring, the careless and indifferent who never darken a church door, let us not forget the selfish people who do darken the church doors, and darken her altars as well!

But prohibition will not prohibit, say some. For that matter, neither does any prohibitory law; the laws against stealing do not entirely prevent stealing; notwithstanding the laws prohibiting murder as set down in the Decalogue, and also in the statute books of our country, there are murders committed. Prohibition will make liquor less accessible. Men may get it still, but it will give them some trouble. In the year 1909 the saloons in the United States were closed at the rate of forty-one a day, and $412,000,000 was the sum that the drink bill decreased. It would seem that prohibition had taken some effect. But, in spite of the mass of evidence, there is still the argument that, under prohibition, there will be much illicit selling of liquor. It will be sold in livery stables and up back lanes, and be carried in coal-oil cans, and labeled 'gopher-poison.' Even so, that will not make it any more deadly in its effects; the effect of liquor-drinking is much the same whether it is drunk in 'the gilded saloon,' where everything is exceedingly legal and regular, or up the back lane, absolutely without authority. Both are bad!

Under prohibition, a drunken man is a marked man – he is branded at once as a law-breaker, and the attitude of the public is that of indignation. Under license, a drunken man is part of the system – and passes without comment. For this reason a small amount of drunkenness in a prohibition territory is so noticeable that many people are deceived into believing that there is more drunkenness under prohibition than under license. Prohibition does not produce drunkenness, but it reveals it, underlines it. Drunkenness in prohibition territory is like a black mark on a white page, a dirty spot on a clean dress; the same spot on a dirty dress would not be noticed.

There was a licensed house in one of the small prairie towns, which complied with all the regulations; it had the required number of bedrooms; its windows were unscreened; the license fee was paid; the bartender was a total abstainer, and a member of the union; also said to be a man of good moral character; the proprietor regularly gave twenty-five dollars a year to the Children's Aid, and put up a cup to be competed for by the district hockey clubs. Nothing could be more regular or respectable, and yet, when men drank the liquor there it had appalling results. There was one Irishman who came frequently to the bar and drank like a gentleman, treating every person and never looking for change from his dollar bill. One Christmas Eve, the drinking went on all night and well into Christmas Day. Then the Irishman, who was the life of the party, went home, remembering what day it was. It all came out in the evidence that he had taken home with him presents for his wife and children, so that his intention toward them was the kindest. His wife's intention was kind, too. She waited dinner for him, and the parcels she had prepared for Christmas presents were beside the plates on the table. For him she had knitted a pair of gray stockings with green rings around them. They were also shown as evidence at the inquest!

It is often claimed that prohibition will produce a lot of sneaking drunkards, but, of course, this man had done his drinking under license, and was of the open and above-board type of drinker. There was nothing underhand or sneaking about him. He drank openly, and when he went home, and his wife asked him why he had stayed away so long, he killed her — not in any underhand or sneaking way. Not at all. Right in the presence of the four little children who had been watching for him all morning at the window, he killed her. When he came to himself, he remembered nothing about it, he said, and those who knew him believed him. A blind pig could not have done much worse for that family! Now, could it?

Years after, when the eldest girl had grown to be a woman, she took sick with typhoid fever and the doctor told her she would die, and she turned her face to the wall and said: 'I am glad.' A friend who stood beside her bed spoke of heaven and the blessed rest that there remains, and the joy of the life everlasting. The girl roused herself and said, bitterly: 'I ask only one thing of heaven and that is, that I may forget the look in my mother's face when she saw he intended to kill her. I do not want to live again. I only want to forget!' The respectability of the house and the legality of the sale did not seem to be any help to her.

But there are people who cry out against prohibition that you cannot make men moral, or sober, by law. But that is exactly what you can do. The greatest value a law has is its moral value. It is the silent pressure of the law on public opinion which gives it its greatest value. The punishment for the infringement of the law is not its only way of impressing itself on the people. It is the moral impact of a law that changes public sentiment, and to say that you cannot make men sober by law is as foolish as to say you cannot keep cattle from destroying the wheat by building a fence between them and it, or to claim you cannot make a crooked twig grow straight by tying it straight. Humanity can do anything it wants to do. There is no limit to human achievement. Whoever declares that things cannot be done which are for the betterment of the race, insults the Creator of us all, who is not willing that any should perish, but that all should live and live abundantly.

Chapter 11

As a man thinketh

When the valley is brimming with sunshine,
   And the Souris, limpid and clear,
Slips over its shining pebbles
   And the harvest time draws near,
The heart of the honest plowman
   Is filled with content and cheer!

It is only the poor, rich farmer
   Whose heart is heavy with dread,
When over the smiling valley
   The mantle of harvest is spread;
'For the season,' he says, 'is backward
   And the grain is only in head!'

The hired man loves the twilight
   When the purple hills grow dim,
And he smiles at the glittering blackbirds
   Which round him circle and skim;
His road is embroidered with sunflowers
   That lazily nod at him!

But the rich man's heart is heavy,
   With gloom and fear opprest;
For he knows the red-winged blackbird
   As an evil-minded pest,
And the golden brown-eyed sunflower
   Is only a weed, at best!

When the purple rain-clouds gather
   And a mist comes over the hills,
A peace beyond all telling
   The hired man's bosom fills,
And the long, long sleep in the morning
   His heart with rapture fills.

But the rich man's heart is heavy
   With gloom and fear of loss,
When the purple clouds drop moisture
   On field and flower and moss;
It's all very well for the plowman,
   But it's not well at all for the 'Boss.'

When the moonlight lies on the valley
   And into the hayloft streams,
Where the humble laborer snoreth
   And dreameth his peaceful dreams;
It silvers his slumbering fancies
   With the witchery of its beams.

But the poor rich man is restless,
   For his heart is on his sheaves;
And the moonlight, cold and cloudless,
   For him no fancy weaves,
For the glass is falling, falling,
   And the grain will surely freeze!

So the poor rich farmer misses
   What makes this old world sweet;
And the weather grieves the heart of him
   With too much rain or heat;
For there's nothing gold that can't be sold,
   And there's nothing good but wheat!

THERE is no class of people who have suffered so much from wrong thinking as the farmer; vicarious wrong thinking, I mean; other people have done the wrong thinking, and the farmer has suffered. Like many another bromide, the thought has grown on people that farmers are slow, uncouth, guileless, easily imposed on, ready to sign a promissory note for any smooth-tongued stranger who comes in for dinner. The stage and the colored supplements have spread this impression of the farmer, and the farmer has not cared. He felt he could stand it! Perhaps the women on the farm feel it more than the men, for women are more sensitive about such things, 'Poor girl!' say the kind friends. 'She went West and married a farmer' – and forthwith a picture of the farmer's wife rises up before their eyes; the poor, faded woman, in a rusty black luster skirt sagging in the back and puckering in the seams; coat that belonged to a suit in other days; a black sailor hat, gray with years and dust, with a sad cluster of faded violets, and torn tulle trimming, sitting crooked on her head; hair the color of last year's grass, and teeth gone in front.

There is no reason for the belief that farmers' wives as a class look and dress like this, only that people love to generalize; to fit cases to their theory, they love to find ministers' sons wild; mothers-in-law disagreeable; women who believe in suffrage neglecting their children, and farmers' wives shabby, discouraged and sad.

I do not believe that farmers' wives are a down-trodden class of women. They have their troubles like other people. It rains in threshing time, and the threshers' visit is prolonged until long after their welcome has been worn to a frazzle! Father won't dress up even when company is coming. Father also has a mania for buying land instead of building a new house; and sometimes works the driving horse. Cows break out of pastures; hawks get the chickens; hens lay away; clothes-lines break.

They have their troubles, but there are compensations. Their houses may be small, but there is plenty of room outside; they may not have much spending money, but the rent is always paid; they are saved from the many disagreeable things that are incident to city life, and they have great opportunity for developing their resources.

When the city woman wants a shelf put up she 'phones to the City Relief, and gets a man to do it for her; the farmer's wife hunts up the hammer and a soap box and puts up her own shelf, and gains the independence of character which only comes from achievement.

Similarly the children of the country neighborhoods have had to make their own fun, which they do with great enthusiasm, for, under any circumstances, children will play. The city children pay for their amusement. They pay their nickel, and sit back, apparently saying: 'Now, amuse me if you can! What are you paid for? The blasé city child who comes sighing out of picture shows is a sad sight. They know everything, and their little souls are a-weary of this world. It is a cold day for any child who has nothing left to wonder at.

The desire to play is surely a great stroke of Providence, and one of which the world has only recently begun to learn. Take the matter of picnics. I have seen people hold a picnic on the bare prairie, where the nearest tree was miles away, and the only shade was that of a barbed-wire fence, but everybody was happy. The success of a picnic depends upon the mental attitude, not on cool shade or purling streams.

I remember seeing from the train window a party of young people carrying a boat and picnic baskets, one hot day in July. A little farther on we passed a tiny lake set in a thick growth of tall grass. It was a very small lake, indeed. I ran to the rear platform of the train and watched it as long as I could; I was so afraid some cow would come along and drink it dry before they got there.

Not long ago I made some investigations as to why boys and girls leave the farm, and I found in over half the cases the reason given was that life on the farm was 'too slow, too lonely, and no fun.' In country neighborhoods family life means more than it does in the city. The members of a family are at each other's mercy; and so, if the 'father' always has a grouch, and the 'mother' is worried, and tired, and cross, small wonder that the children try to get away. In the city there is always the 'movie' to go to, and congenial companionship down the street, and so we mourn the depopulation of our rural neighborhoods.

We all know that the country is the best place in which to bring up children; that the freckle-faced boy, with bare feet, who hunts up the cows after school, and has to keep the woodbox full, and has to remember to shut the henhouse door, is getting a far better education than the carefree city boy who has everything done for him.

It is a good thing that boys leave the farm and go to the city — I mean it is a good thing for the city — but it is hard on the farm. Of

late years this question has become very serious and has caused
alarm. Settlements which, ten or fifteen years ago, had many young
people and a well-filled school and well-attended church, with the
real owners living on the farms, have now become depopulated by
farmers retiring to a nearby town and 'renters' taking the place.
'Renters' are very often very poor, and sometimes shiftless – no
money to spend on anything but the real necessities; sometimes even
too poor to send their children to school.

One cause for this is that our whole attitude toward labor is
wrong. We look upon labor as an uncomfortable experience, which,
if we endure with patience, we may hope to outgrow and be able to
get away from. We practically say: 'Let us work now, so that by and
by we may be able to live without working!' Many a farmer and his
wife have denied themselves everything for years, comforting
themselves with the thought that when they have enough money
they will 'retire.' They will not take the time or the money to go to
a concert, or a lecture, or a picnic, but tell themselves that when
they retire they will just go to everything. So just when they have
everything in fine shape on the farm, when the lilacs are beginning to
bloom and the raspberry bushes are bearing, they 'retire.' Father's
rheumatism is bad, and mother can't get help, so they rent the farm
and retire.

The people to whom the farm is rented do not care anything
about the lilac or raspberry bushes – there is no money in them. All
they care about is wheat – they have to pay the rent and they want
to make money. They have the wheat lust, so the lilacs bloom or not
as they feel disposed, and the cattle trample down the raspberry
bushes and the gate falls off the top hinge. Meanwhile the farmer
and his wife move into town and buy a house. They get just a small
house, for the wife says she's tired of working. Every morning at
4.30 o'clock they waken. They often thought about how nice it
would be not to have to get up; but now, someway it isn't nice.
They can't sleep, everything is so quiet. Not a rooster crowing. Nor a
hen cackling! They get up and look out. All down the street the
blinds are drawn. Everybody is asleep – and it all looks so blamed
lazy.

They get up. But there is nothing to do. The woman is not so
badly off – a woman can always tease out linen and sew it up again,
and she can always crochet. Give her a crochet needle, and a spool of
'sil-cotton,' and she will keep out of mischief. But the man is not so

easy to account for. He tries hard to get busy. He spades the garden as if he were looking for diamonds. He cleans the horse until the poor brute hates the sight of him. He piles his wood so carefully that the neighbors passing call out and ask him if he 'intends to varnish it.' He mends everything that needs it, and is glad when he finds a picket off the fence. He tries to read the *Farmers' Advocate*. They brought in a year's number of them that they had never got time to read on the farm. Someway, they have lost their charm. It seems so lazy in broad daylight for a grown man to sit down and read. He takes a walk downtown, and meets up with some idle men like himself. They sit on the sidewalk and settle the government and the church and various things.

'Well, I must be gittin'!' at last he declares; then suddenly he remembers that he has nothing to do at home — everything is done to a finish — and a queer, detached feeling comes over him. He is no longer needed anywhere.

Somebody is asking him to come in for a drink, and he goes! Why shouldn't he have a drink or anything else that he wants, he asks himself. He has worked hard. He'll take two. He'll go even further, he'll treat the crowd. When he finally goes home and sleeps it off, he finds he has spent $1.05, and he is repentant.

That night a young lady calls, selling tickets for a concert, and his wife would have bought them, but he says: 'Go slow, Minnie, you can't buy everything. It's awful the way money goes in town. We'll see about this concert — maybe we'll go, but we won't buy tickets — it might rain!'

They do not buy the tickets — neither do they go. Minnie does not care much about going out. She has stayed in too long. But he continues to sit on the sidewalk, and he hears many things.

Sometimes people have attributed to women the habit of gossiping, but the idle men, who sit on the sidewalks of the small towns or tilt back in the yellow round-back chairs on the hotel verandas, can blacken more characters to the hour than any other class of human beings. He hears all the putrid stories of the little town; they are turned over and discussed in all their obnoxious details. At first, he is repelled by them, for he is a decent fellow, this man who put in the lilacs and the raspberry bushes back there on the farm. He objects to the remarks that are passed about the women who go by, and he says so, and he and one of the other men have 'words.'

The bartender hears it and comes out and settles it by inviting everyone in to have 'one on the house.'

That brings back good-fellowship, and everyone treats. He sees then that nobody meant any harm – it was all just in fun. A few glasses of 'White Horse' will keep a man from being too sensitive about things. So he laughs with the others at the indecent joke. This is life – town life. Now he is out in the world!

So begins the degeneration of a man, and it is all based on the false attitude we have toward labor. His idea of labor was wrong while he was on the farm. He worked and did nothing else, until he forgot how to do everything else. Then he stopped working, and he was lost.

Why any rational human being wants to 'retire' to the city, goes beyond me! I can understand the city man, worn with the noise, choked by the dust, frazzled with cares, retiring to the country, where he can heal his tired soul, pottering around his own garden, and watching green things grow. That seems reasonable and logical! But for a man who has known the delight of planting and reaping to retire to a city or a small town, and 'hang around,' doing nothing, is surely a retrograde step.

The retired farmer is seldom interested in community matters – they usually vote against any by-law for improvement. Coal-oil lamps were good enough on the farm – why should a town have electric light? Why should a town spend money on cement sidewalks when they already have good dirt roads? He will not subscribe funds for the support of a gymnasium, hockey club or public baths. He does not understand about the need of exercise, he always got too much; and he doesn't see any reason why the boys should not go to the river and swim.

It is not that the farmer is selfish or mean above or below other men. It is because he has not learned team play or the community spirit. But it is coming. The farmer has been an independent fellow, able to get along without much help from anyone. He could always hire plenty of men, and there are machines for every need. So far as the farmer has been concerned, he could get along very well.

It has not been so with the farmer's wife. More than any other woman she has needed help, and less than any other woman has she got it. She has been left alone, to live or die, sink or swim.

Machines for helping the man on the farm are on the market in great numbers, and are bought eagerly, for the farmer reasons out the matter quite logically, and arrives at the conclusion that anything which will add to the productiveness of his farm is good buying. He can see the financial value of a seeder, or a roller, or a feed chopper. Now, with a washing-machine it is different. A washing-machine can only wash clothes, and his wife has always been able to get the clothes washed some way. The farmer does not see any return for his ten dollars and a half, and so he passes up the machine. Besides this, his mother never used one, and always managed to keep the clothes clean, too, and that settles it!

The outside farm work has progressed wonderfully, but the indoor farm work is done in exactly the same way as it was twenty-five years ago, with the possible exception of the cream-separator.

Many a farmyard, with its binders, rakes, drills, rollers, gasoline engine, fanning-mill, and steam-plow looks as if someone had been giving a machinery shower; but in the kitchen you will find the old washboard and dasher churn, which belonged to the same era as the reaping hook and tallow candle. The women still carry the water in a pail from a pump outside, wash the dishes on the kitchen table, and carry the water out again in a pail; although out in the barn the water is pumped by a windmill, or a gasoline engine. The outside work on the farm is done by horse, steam, or gasoline, but the indoor work is all done by woman-power.

And then, when the woman-power gives out, as it does many times, under the strain of hard work and childbearing, the whole neighborhood mourns and says: 'God's ways are past finding out.'

I remember once attending the funeral of a woman who had been doing the work for a family of six children and three hired men, and she had not even a baby carriage to make her work lighter. When the last baby was three days old, just in threshing time, she died. Suddenly, and without warning, the power went off, and she quit without notice. The bereaved husband was the most astonished man in the world. He had never known Jane to do a thing like that before, and he could not get over it. In threshing time, too!

'I don't know what could have happened to Jane — a strong young woman like her,' he said over and over again.

We all gathered at the house that afternoon and paid our respects to the deceased sister, and we were all very sorry for poor Ed. We said it was a terrible way for a poor man to be left.

The chickens came close to the dining-room door, and looked in, inquisitively. They could not understand why she did not come out and feed them, and when they were driven away they retreated in evident bad humor, gossiping openly of the shiftless, lazy ways of folks they could mention, if they wished to name names.

The six little children, whom the neighbor women had dressed in their best clothes, sat dazed and silent, fascinated by the draped black coffin; but the baby, the tiny one who had just entered the race, gathered up the feeling of the meeting, and cried incessantly in a room upstairs. It was a hard rebellious cry, too, as if the little one realized that an injustice had been done.

Just above the coffin hung an enlarged picture of 'Jane' in her wedding dress, and it was a bright face that looked out at the world from the heavy gold frame, a sweet girlish face, which seemed to ask a question with its eager eyes. And there below, in the black draped coffin, was the answer — the same face, only a few years older, but tired, so inexpressibly tired, cold and silent; its light gone out — the power gone off. Jane had been given her answer. And upstairs Jane's baby cried its bitter, insistent cry.

Just then the minister began to read the words of the funeral service:

'Inasmuch as it hath *pleased* the Lord . . .'

This happened in the fall of the year, and the next spring, just before the busy time came on, the bereaved husband dried his eyes, painted his buggy, and went out and married one of the neighbor's daughters, a good strong one — and so his house is still running on woman-power.

If men had to bear the pain and weariness of childbearing, in addition to the unending labors of housework and caring for children, for one year, at the end of that time there would be a perfect system of cooperation and labor-saving devices in operation, for men have not the genius for martyrdom that women have; and they know the value of coöperative labor. No man tries to do everything the way women do. No man aspires to making his own clothes, cleaning his own office, pressing his own suits, or even cleaning his own shoes. All these things he is quite willing to let people do for him, while he goes ahead and does his own work. Man's work is systematized well and leaves a man free to work in his own way. His days are not broken up by details.

On the other hand the home is the most haphazard institution we have. Everything is done there. (I am speaking now of the homes in the country.) In each of the homes there is a little bit of washing done, a little dressmaking, a little butter-making, a little baking, a little ironing going on, and it is all by handpower, which is the most expensive power known. It is also being done largely by amateurs, and that adds to the amount of labor expended. Women have worked away at these endless tasks for generations, lovingly, unselfishly, doing their level best to do everything, with no thought of themselves at all. When things get too many for them, and the burdens overpower them, they die quietly, and some other woman, young, strong and fresh, takes their place, and the modest white slab in the graveyard says 'Thy will be done,' and everybody is apparently satisfied. The Lord is blamed for the whole thing.

Now, if men, with their good organizing ability and their love of comfort and their sense of their own importance, were set down to do the work that women have done all down the centuries, they would evolve a scheme something like this in each of the country neighborhoods. There would be a central station, municipally owned and operated, one large building fitted out with machinery that would be run by gasoline, electricity, or natural gas. This building would contain in addition to the school-rooms, a laundry room, a bake-shop, a creamery, a dressmaking establishment, and perhaps a butcher shop.

The consolidated school and the 'Beef-rings' in the country district are already established facts, and have opened the way for this larger scheme of coöperation. In this manner the work would be done by experts, and in the cheapest way, leaving the women in the farm homes with time and strength to raise their children.

This plan would solve the problem, too, of young people leaving the farm. Many of the young people would find occupation in the central station and become proficient in some branch of the work carried on there. They would find not only employment, but the companionship of people of their own age. The central station would become a social gathering place in the evenings for all the people of the district, and it is not too visionary to see in it a lecture hall, a moving-picture machine, and a music room. Then the young people would be kept on the farms because their homes would be pleasanter places. No woman can bake, wash, scrub, cook meals and raise children and still be happy. To do all these things would make an archangel irritable, and no home can be happy when the poor mother is too tired to smile! The children feel an atmosphere of gloom, and naturally get away from it as soon as they can. The over-worked mother cannot make the home attractive; the things that can be left undone are left undone, and so the cushions on the lounge are dirty and torn, the pictures hang crooked on the walls, and the hall lamp has had no oil in it for months. That does not matter, though, for the family live in the kitchen, and, during the winter, the other part of the house is of the same temperature as a well. Knowing that she is not keeping her house as it should be kept has taken the heart out of many a woman on the farm. But what can she do? The meals have to be cooked; the butter must be made!

There are certain burdens which could be removed from the women on the farm; there is part of their work that could be done cheaper and better elsewhere, and the whole farm and all its people would reap the benefit.

But right about here I think I hear from Brother Bones of Bonesville:

'Do you mean to say that we should pay for the washing, ironing, bread-making, sewing?' he cries out. 'We never could afford it, and, besides, what would the women put in their time at if all that work was done for them?'

Brother Bones, we can always afford to pay for things in money rather than in human flesh and blood. That is the most exorbitant price the race can pay for anything, and we have been paying for farm work that way for a long time. If you doubt this statement, I can show you the receipts which have been chiseled in stone and marble in every graveyard.

SACRED TO THE MEMORY
OF
JANE
BELOVED WIFE OF EDWARD JAMES
AGED 32 YEARS AND 6 MONTHS

Who can estimate the worth of a mother to her family and the community?

An old widower, who was reproved for marrying a very young girl for his third wife, exonerated himself from blame by saying: 'It would ruin any man to be always buryin', and buryin'.'

But Brother Bones is not yet satisfied, and he is sure the women will have nothing to do if such a scheme would be followed out, and he tells us that his mother always did these things herself and raised her family, too.

'I can tell you,' says Brother Bones, 'my mother knew something about rearing children; she raised seven and buried seven, and she never lay in bed for more than three days with any of them. Poor mother, she was a very smart woman — at least so I have been told — I don't remember her.'

That's just the point, Brother Bones. It is a great thing to have the memory of such a self-sacrificing mother, but it would be a greater thing to have your mother live out her days; and then, too, we are thinking of the 'seven' she buried. That seems like a wicked and unnecessary waste of young life, of which we should feel profoundly ashamed. Poor little people, who came into life, tired and weak, fretfully complaining, burdened already with the cares of the world and its unending labor —

Your old earth, they say, is very weary;
Our young feet, they say, are very weak,

and when the measles or whooping-cough assails them they have no strength to battle with it, and so they pass out, and again the Lord is blamed!

It is very desirable for the world that people should be born and brought up in the country with its honest, wholesome ways learned in the open; its habits of meditation, which have grown on the people as they have gone about their work in the quiet places. Thought currents in the country are strong and virile, and flow freely. There is an honesty of purpose in the man who strikes out the long furrow, and turns over every inch of the sod, painstakingly and without pretense; for he knows that he cannot cheat nature; he will get back what he puts in; he will reap what he sows — for Nature has no favorites, and no short-cuts, nor can she be deceived, fooled, cajoled or flattered.

We need the unaffected honesty and sterling qualities which the country teaches her children in the hard, but successful, school of experience, to offset the flashy supercilious lessons which the city teaches hers; for the city is a careless nurse and teacher, who thinks more of the cut of a coat than of the habit of mind; who feeds her children on colored candy and popcorn, despising the more wholesome porridge and milk; a slatternly nurse, who would rather buy perfume than soap; who allows her children to powder their necks instead of washing them; who decks them out in imitation lace collars, and cheap jewelry, with bows on their hair, but holes in their stockings; who dazzles their eyes with bright lights and commercial signs, and fills their ears with blatant music, until their eyes are too dull to see the pastel beauty of common things, and their ears are holden to the still small voices of God; who lures her children on with many glittering promises of ease and wealth, which she never intends to keep, and all the time whispers to them that this is life.

The good old country nurse is stern but kind, and gives her children hard lessons, which tax body and brain, but never fail to bring a great reward. She sends them on long journeys, facing the piercing winter winds, but rewards them when the journey is over with rosy cheeks and contented mind, and an appetite that is worth going miles to see; and although she makes her children work long hours, until their muscles ache, she gives them, for reward, sweet sleep and pleasant dreams; and sometimes there are the sweet surprises along life's highway; the sudden song of birds or burst of sunshine; the glory of the sunrise, and sunset, and the flash of bluebirds' wings across the road, and the smell of the good green earth.

Happy is the child who learns earth's wisdom from the good old country nurse, who does better than she promises, and always 'makes her children mind'!

Chapter 12

The war against gloom

Not for all sunshine, dear Lord, do we pray —
   We know such a prayer would be vain;
But that strength may be ours to keep right on our way,
   Never minding the rain!

IT IS a great thing to be young, when every vein throbs with energy and life, when the rhythm of life beats its measures into our hearts and calls upon us to keep step with Joy and Gladness, as we march confidently down the white road which leads to the Land of Desire. God made every young thing to be happy. He put joy and harmony into every little creature's heart. Who ever saw a kitten with a grouch? Or a little puppy who was a pessimist? But you have seen sad children a-plenty, and we are not blaming the Almighty for that either. God's plans have been all right, but they have been badly interfered with by human beings.

When a young colt gallops around the corral, kicking and capering and making a good bit of a nuisance of himself, the old horses watch him sympathetically, and very tolerantly. They never say: 'It is well for you that you can be so happy – you'll have your troubles soon enough. Childhood is your happiest time – you do well to enjoy it, for there's plenty of trouble ahead of you!'

Horses never talk this way. This is a distinctively human way of depressing the young. People do it from a morbid sense of duty. They feel that mirth and laughter are foreign to our nature, and should be curbed as something almost wicked.

'It's a fine day, today!' we admit grudgingly, 'but, look out! We'll pay up for it!'

'I have been very well all winter, but I must not boast. Touch wood!'

The inference here is that when we are healthy or happy or enjoying a fine day, we are in an abnormal condition. We are getting away with a bit of happiness that is not intended for us. God is not noticing, and we had better go slow and keep dark about it, or He will waken up with a start, and send us back to our aches and pains and our dull leaden skies! Thus have we sought to sow the seeds of despondency and unbelief in the world around us.

In the South African War, there was a man who sowed the seeds of despondency among the British soldiers; he simply talked defeat and disaster, and so greatly did he damage the morale of the troops that an investigation had to be made, and as a result the man was sent to jail for a year. People have been a long time learning that thoughts are things to heal, upbuild, strengthen; or to wound, impair, or blight. After all we cannot do very much for many people, no matter how hard we try, but we can contribute to their usefulness and happiness by holding for them a kind thought if we will.

There are people who depress you so utterly that if you had to remain under their influence they would rob you of all your ambition and initiative, while others inspire you to do better, to achieve, to launch out. Life is made up of currents of thought as real as are the currents of air, and if we could but see them, there are currents of thought we would avoid as we would smallpox germs.

Sadness is not our normal mental condition, nor is weakness our normal physical condition. God intended us to laugh and play and work, come to our beds at night weary and ready to sleep – and wake refreshed.

'As a man thinketh in his heart, so is he!' No truer words were ever spoken, and yet men try to define themselves by houses and lands and manners and social position, but all to no avail. The old rule holds. It is your thought which determines what manner of man you are. The respectable man who keeps within the law and does no outward harm, but who thinks sordidly, meanly, or impurely, is the man of all others who is farthest from the kingdom of God, because he does not feel his need, nor can anyone help him. Thoughts are harder to change than ways.

'Let the wicked man forsake his ways, and the unrighteous man his thoughts,' declared Isaiah long ago, and there is no doubt the unrighteous man has the hardest and biggest proposition put up to him.

When the power of thought is understood, there will be a change in our newspapers. Now the tendency is to ignore the good in life and underline the evil in red ink. If a man commits a theft, it will make a newspaper story, bought and paid for at regular rates. If it is a very big steal, you may wire it in and get telegraphic rates. If the thief shoots a man, too, send along his picture and you may make the story two columns. If he shoots two or three people, you may give him the whole front page, and somebody will write a book about him. It will sell, too. How much more wholesome would our newspapers be, if they published the good deeds of men and women rather than their misdoings. Why should not as much space be given to the man who saves a life, as is given to the man who takes a life? Why not let us hear more of the boy who went right, rather than of the one who went wrong? I remember once reading an obscure little paragraph about a man who every year a few days before Christmas sent twenty-five dollars to the Postal Department at Ottawa, to pay the deficit on Christmas parcels which were held up for insufficient postage. Such a thoughtful act of Christian charity should have been given a place on the front page, for in the words of Jennie Allen: 'Life ain't any too full of nice little surprises like that.' Why should people enjoy the contemplation of evil rather than good? Is it because it makes their own little contribution of respectability seem larger by comparison?

We have missed a great deal of the joy of life by taking ourselves too seriously. We exaggerate our own importance, and so if the honor or distinction or the vote of thanks does not come our way, we are hurt! Then, too, we live in an atmosphere of dread and fear — we fear poverty and hard work — we fear the newspapers and the neighbors, and fear is hell!

When you begin to feel all fussed up, worried, and cross, frayed at the edges, and down at the heel — go out and look up at the stars. They are so serene, detached, and uncaring! Calmly shining down upon us they rebuke the fussiness of our little souls, and tell us to cheer up, for our little affairs do not much matter anyway.

> The earthly hope men set their hearts upon
> Turns ashes, or it prospers — and anon
> Like snow upon the desert's arid face,
> Cooling a little hour or two — is gone!

It is a great mistake for us to mistake ourselves for the President of the company. Let us do our little bit with cheerfulness and not take the responsibility that belongs to God. None of us can turn the earth around; all we can ever hope to do is to hit it a few whacks on the right side. We belong to a great system; a system which can convince even the dullest of us of its greatness. Think of the miracle of night and day enacted before our eyes every twenty-four hours. Right on the dot comes the sun up over the saucer-like rim of the earth, never a minute late. Think of the journey the earth makes around the sun every year — a matter of 360,000,000 miles more or less — and it makes the journey in an exact time and arrives on the stroke of the clock, no washout on the line; no hot box; no spread rail; no taking on of coal or water; no employees' strike. It never drops a stick; it never slips a cog; and whirls in through space always on the minute. And that without any help from either you or me! Some system, isn't it?

I believe we may safely trust God even with our affairs. When the war broke out we all experienced a bad attack of gloom. We were afraid God had forgotten us and gone off the job. And yet, even now, we begin to see light through the dark clouds of sorrow and confusion. If the war brings about the abolition of the liquor traffic, it will be justified. Incidentally the war has already brought many by-products which are wholly good, and it would almost seem as if there is a plan in it after all.

Life is a great struggle against gloom, and we could fight it better if we always remembered that happiness is a condition of heart and is not dependent on outward conditions. The kingdom of heaven is within you. Everything depends on the point of view.

> Two prisoners looked out once through the bars,
> One saw the mud, the other saw the stars.

Looking into the sky one sees the dark clouds and foretells rain, and the picnic spoiled; another sees the rift of blue and foretells fine weather. Looking out on life, one sees only its sad grayness; another sees the thread of gold, 'which sometimes in the patterns shows most sweet where there are somber colors'! Happiness is a condition, and if you are not happy now, you had better be alarmed about yourself, for you may never be.

There was a woman who came with her family to the prairie country thirty-five years ago. They built a house, which in those days of sod roofs and Red-River frames seemed quite palatial, for had it not a 'parlor' and a pantry and three bedrooms? The lady grieved and mourned incessantly because it had no back-stairs. In ten years they built another house, and it had everything, back-stairs, dumb-waiter, and laundry shoot, and all the neighbors wondered if the lady would be happy then. She wasn't. She wanted to live in the city. She had the good house now and that part of her discontent was closed down, so it broke out in another place. She hated the country. By diligently keeping at it, she induced her husband to go to the city where the poor man was about as much at home as a sailor at a dry-farming congress. He made no complaint, however. The complaint department was always busy! She suddenly discovered that a Western city was not what she wanted. It was 'down East.' So they went. They bought a beautiful home in the orchard country in Ontario, and her old neighbors watched development. Surely she had found peace at last — but she hadn't. She did not like the people — she missed the friendliness of the new country; also she objected to the winters, and her dining-room was dark, and the linen closet was small. Soon after moving to Ontario she died, and we presume went to heaven. It does not matter where she went — she won't like it anyway. She had the habit of discontent.

There's no use looking ahead for happiness — look around! If it is anywhere, it is here.

'I am going out to bring in some apples to eat,' said a farmer to his wife.

'Mind you bring in the spotted ones,' said she who had a frugal mind.

'What'll I do if there are no spotted ones?' he asked.

'Don't bring any — just wait until they do spot!'

Too many people do not eat their apples until they are spotted.

But we know that life has its tragedies, its heartaches, its gloom, in spite of all our philosophy. We may as well admit it. We have no reason to believe that we shall escape, but we have reason to hope that when these things come to us we will be able to bear them.

'Thou shalt not be *afraid* of the terror by day, nor of the arrow that flieth by night, nor for the pestilence that walketh in darkness, nor for the destruction that wasteth at noonday.'

You will notice here that the promise is that you will not be *afraid* of these things. They may come to you, but they will not overpower you, or destroy you utterly, for you will not be afraid of them. It is fear that kills. It is better to have misfortunes come, and be brave to meet them, than to be afraid of them all your life, even if they never come.

Gloom and doubt and fear paralyze the soul and sow it thick with the seeds of defeat. No man is a failure until he admits it himself.

Tramps have a way of marking gateposts so that their companions who may come along afterwards may know exactly what sort of people live inside, and whether it is worth while to ask them for a meal. A certain sign means 'Easy people — no questions'; another sign means 'Nothing stirring — don't go in'; another means 'Beat it or they'll give you a job with lots of advice!' and still another means 'Dog.' Every doubt and fear that enters your heart, or tries to enter, leaves its mark upon the gatepost of your soul, and it serves as a guide for every other doubt and fear which may come along, and if they once mark you 'Easy,' that signal will act as an invitation for their twin brother 'Defeat,' who will, without warning, slip into your heart and make himself at home.

Doubts and fears are disloyalty to God — they are expressions of a want of confidence in Him, but, of course, that's what is wrong with our religion. We have not got enough of it. Too many of us have just enough religion to make ourselves miserable — just enough to spoil our taste for worldly pleasures and not enough to give us a taste for the real things of life. There are many good qualities which are only an aggravation if we have not enough of them. 'Every good and perfect gift cometh from above.' You see it is not enough for the gift to be 'good' — it must be 'perfect,' and that means abundant. Too long we have thought of religion as something in the nature of straight life insurance — we would have to die to get the good of it. But it isn't. The good of it is here, and now we can 'lift' it every day if we will. No person can claim wages for half time; that's where so much dissatisfaction has come in, and people have found fault with the company. People have taken up the service of God as a polite little side-line and worked at it when they felt like it — Sunday afternoons perhaps or rainy days, when there was nothing else going on; and then when no reward came — no peace of soul — they were disposed to grumble. They were like plenty of policy-holders and did not read the contract, or perhaps some agent had in the excess of his zeal made it too easy for them. The reward comes only when you put your whole strength on all the time. Out in the Middle West they have a way of making the cattle pump their own water by a sort of platform, which the weight of an animal will press down, and the water is forced up into a trough. Sometimes a blasé old ox who sees the younger and lighter steers doing this, feels that he with his superior experience and weight will only have to put one foot on to bring up the water, but he finds that one foot won't do, or even two. He has to get right on, and give to it his full weight. It takes the whole ox, horns, hoofs and tail. That's the way it is in religion — by which we mean the service of God and man. It takes you — all the time; and the reward is work, and peace, and a satisfaction in your work that passeth all understanding. No more grinding fear, no more 'bad days,' no more wishing to die, no more nervous prostration. Just work and peace!

Did you ever have to keep house when your mother went away, when you did not know very well how to do things, and every meal sat like a weight on your young heart, and the fear was ever present with you that the bread would go sour or the house burn down, or burglars would come, or someone would take sick? The days were like years as they slowly crawled around the face of the old clock on the kitchen shelf, and even at night you could not forget the awful burden of responsibility.

But one day, one glorious day she came home, and the very minute you heard her step on the floor, the burden was lifted. Your work was very much the same, but the responsibility was gone, and cheerfulness came back to your eyes, and smiles to your face.

That is what it feels like when you 'get religion.' The worry and burden of life is gone. Somebody else has the responsibility and you work with a light heart. It is the responsibility of life that kills us, the worry, fear, uncertainty, and anxiety. How we envy the man who works by the day, just does his little bit, and has no care! This immunity from care may be ours if we link ourselves with God.

Think of Moses' mother! There she was hired to take care of her own son. Doing the very thing she loved to do all week and getting her pay envelope every Saturday night. So may we. God hires us to do our work for Him, and pays us as we go along – the only stipulation being that we do our best.

'I have shown thee, O man, what is good!' declared Micah long ago. 'What doth now the Lord require of thee, but to do justly, to love mercy and walk humbly with thy God!' In 'walking humbly, doing justly, and loving mercy,' there is no place for worry and gloom; there is great possibility of love and much serving, and God in His goodness breaks up our reward into a thousand little things which attend us every step of the way, just as the white ray of light by the drop of water is broken into the dazzling beauty of the rainbow. The burning bush which Moses saw is not the only bush which flames with God, and seeks to show to us a sign. Nature spares no pains to make things beautiful; trees have serrated leaves; birds and flowers have color; the butterflies' wings are splashed with gold; moss grows over the fallen tree, and grass covers the scar on the landscape. Nature hides her wounds in beauty. Nature spares no pains to make things beautiful, for beauty is nourishing. Beauty is thrift, ugliness is waste, ugliness is sin which scatters, destroys, integrates. But beauty heals, nourishes, sustains. There is a reason for sending flowers to the sick.

Nature has no place for sadness and repining. The last leaf on the tree dances in the breezes as merrily as when it had all its lovely companions by its side, and when its hold is loosened on the branch which bares it, it joins its brothers on the ground without regret. When the seed falls into the ground and dies, it does it without a murmur, for it knows that it will rise again in new beauty. Happy indeed is the traveler on life's highway, who will read the messages God sends us every day, for they are many and their meaning is clear: the sudden flood of warm sunshine in your room on a dark and dreary afternoon; the billowy softness of the smoke plume which rises into the frosty air, and is touched into exquisite rose and gold by the morning sun; the frosted leaves which turn to crimson and gold — God's silent witnesses that sorrow, disappointment and loss may bring out the deeper beauties of the soul; the flash of a bluebird's wing as he rides gaily down the wind into the sunlit valley. All these are messages to you and me that all is well — letters from home, good comrade, letters from home!

God knew that some would never look
  Inside a book
  To know His will,
And so He threw a varied hue
  On dale and hill.
He knew that some would read words wrong,
And so He gave the birds their song.
  He put the gold in the sunset sky
  To show us that a day may die
  With greater glory than it's born,
    And so may we
  Move calmly forward to our West,
    Serene and blest!